Pages of Enlightenment

開
悟
一
片
片

by Sheng-yen Lu

Translated by Lianhua Zhiwei

A US Daden Culture Publication

US Daden Culture LLC
3440 Foothill Blvd.
Oakland, CA 94601
U.S.A.
Website: www.usdaden.com
Email: us.daden.culture@gmail.com

Lu, Sheng-yen, 1945-
Pages of Enlightenment/by Sheng-yen Lu;
translated by Lianhua Zhiwei;
edited by Alice Yang;
proofread by Renee Cordsen.

Library of Congress Control Number (PCN): 2012938870
ISBN-13: 978-0-9841561-5-3
ISBN-10: 0-9841561-5-1
1. True Buddha School. 2. Chinese-Tibetan Buddhism.
Cover design and layout by US Daden Culture Design Team
Photograph by US Daden Culture
Set in Minion Pro 12
US Daden books are printed on acid-free paper and meet the guidelines for the permanence and durability set by the Council of Library Resources.

Printed in U.S.A.

ISBN 978-0-9841561-5-3
51200>

9 780984 156153

Special Acknowledgements

The True Buddha Translation Teams (TBTTs) would like to express the highest honor and deepest gratitude to Living Buddha Lian-sheng, Sheng-yen Lu, and Master Lianxiang for their continuing support and guidance on the translation effort. Without their compassion, wisdom, blessings, and encouragement, this project would not have reached fruition.

In addition, we would like to acknowledge the diligent work put forth by the following volunteers on this project: Lianhua Zhiwei (translator), Alice Yang (editor), Renee Cordsen (proofreader and desk-top publishing), Gia Tran (quality control). We would like to thank these dedicated and selfless volunteers who have contributed their time and effort to promote the works of Living Buddha Lian-sheng, and to support the publications of the US Daden Culture.

We would also like to extend our sincere appreciation to all of the other volunteers who work behind the scenes, facilitating the translation process, and handling administrative responsibilities.

May all volunteers be blessed for their immeasurable merits; may all sentient beings benefit from the ocean of wisdom.

Table of Contents

To be honest, there are only three types of people who call themselves enlightened: Crazies, the truly enlightened, and con-artists. I am neither crazy nor am I a con-artist. I am truly enlightened.

Sheng-yen Lu

Preface: Profoundly Sublime, Profoundly Sublime, the Most Profoundly Sublime

While enlightenment is a general and often used term, enlightened beings are uncommon and rare. Hence, I have called the preface of this book "Profoundly Sublime, Profoundly Sublime, the Most Profoundly Sublime." Despite being a familiar term, enlightenment is not a state many people reach. Although I described enlightenment as a "state," it doesn't have any state in actuality. The word "state" is only symbolic.

One of the disparaging comments frequently made against me is, "Claiming realization and attainment without achieving either," which is to say that Sheng-yen Lu hasn't achieved enlightenment or Living Buddha Lian-sheng hasn't attained realization. I don't need to defend myself because I understand that enlightenment is profoundly difficult to comprehend. In fact, nobody can understand or decipher my *Pages of Enlightenment*. Some people may have practiced with incredible dedication for a long time, overcame great hardships, and read through all of the scriptures. Yet, it is still extremely difficult for them to get even a glimpse of my realization.

So, am I saying that I, Living Buddha Lian-sheng, Sheng-yen Lu, am the greatest person in this world? Am I saying that I am truly successful in life? Am I saying that I am the only person who is enlightened on this Earth? Am I saying that no other person in this world has achieved enlightenment? Is that right? To be honest, there are only three types of people who call themselves enlightened: Crazies, the truly enlightened, and con-artists. I am neither crazy nor am I a con-artist. I am truly enlightened. All the enlightened ones are the greatest people in the world, the true gurus of life. I am not the only person who has achieved enlightenment on this Earth. But, I see very few genuinely enlightened ones in this world. They are only a handful in number.

World-renown masters are not necessarily enlightened!

Masters with great numbers of students are not necessarily enlightened!

Zen masters who have established the largest temples and monasteries are not necessarily enlightened!

The foremost experts on the scriptures are not necessarily enlightened!

Great masters of the Yogacara School are not necessarily enlightened!

Elders of the Madhyamaka School are not necessarily enlightened!

The greatest living buddhas of the world are not necessarily enlightened!

The most famous vajra masters of the world are not necessarily enlightened!

The great dharma kings of Vajrayana are not necessarily enlightened!

Practitioners all over the world will mercilessly disparage me for writing the above comments, saying Sheng-yen Lu is such a trouble-maker! Sheng-yen Lu is such a bastard! Sheng-yen Lu is an evil heathen! Sheng-yen Lu is a phony, fraudulent, bogus, and fake living buddha! Am I the real deal or a fraud? Please read this book!

Have I really attained enlightenment or is my enlightenment fake? Please read this book! If you would like to get a glimpse at the most profoundly sublime, please see who I really am! Please read this book! This book is guaranteed to be astonishing.

Living Buddha Lian-sheng Sheng-yen Lu's contact information:

Sheng-yen Lu
17102 NE 40th Ct.
Redmond, WA 98052
U.S.A.

I am willing to help you to achieve enlightenment. Have you figured it out? If you haven't figured it out, please continue reading. I will certainly reveal "it."

Sheng-yen Lu

1. Direct Revelation

There is an arrogant man who has led his out-spoken followers into disparaging various aspects of dharma teachings and criticizing past and present-day teachers. Being the author of several books, he regards himself as truly enlightened. Based on my observations, he has not necessarily achieved realization!

I also read the book, *Immediate Enlightenment* by Supreme Master Ching Hai. It made me laugh! I read the book out of curiosity, wondering how there could be a book on "immediate enlightenment." I feel that Supreme Master Ching Hai's thinking is very progressive. However, has she achieved enlightenment? I reserve my opinion. Ha! I am not answering that question.

What cannot be denied is that Shakyamuni Buddha (the World Honored One) attained genuine perfect enlightenment. The Buddhist scriptures are divided into two classes of conventional truth (partial revelation of truth) and absolute truth (total revelation of ultimate reality). There are so many Buddhist scriptures in the Tripitaka [the Buddhist Canon] that if you try to read them all you will have grown a long beard by the time you finish. But, those are only the scriptures revealed to humanity. There are even more scriptures hidden in the palaces of the nagas that have never been seen by the people of this world.

Why am I certain that the World Honored One, Lord Buddha, achieved true perfect enlightenment? I am certain because of the Buddha's three key statements:

1. Inexpressible.
2. Never spoke a word.
3. There is no Dharma to teach, and I have never taught any Dharma.

Hence, it is affirmative that Shakyamuni Buddha is genuinely enlightened.

After reading the passages above, many Buddhists might exclaim: "Who does Sheng-yen Lu think he is? He is truly outlandish and has disrespected the Buddha. How dare anyone judge whether or not Lord Buddha himself is enlightened or not? This Sheng-yen Lu person really should go to hell!"

I politely request all Buddhists to calm down and not to be in such a rush to disparage me. Who am I really? I had coffee with the World Honored One, and we travelled on trips together. I have the greatest respect for the World Honored One and nobody needs to doubt that. What the World Honored One taught is not something that can be thoroughly understood by cursory examination. Some of the teachings are so profound that you have no idea what the World Honored One meant or really said. Yet, if you use your wisdom eye, then you will slowly understand the true meaning of his teachings.

Think it over:

1. Inexpressible.
2. Never spoke a word.
3. There is no Dharma to teach, and I have never taught any Dharma.

Enlightenment, what is it? It is concealed in these three statements. You should carefully contemplate them. I am willing to help you to achieve enlightenment. Have you figured it out? If you haven't figured it out, please continue reading. I will certainly reveal "it."

> No matter if it is alive,
> No matter if it is dead,
> Everything is part of this boundless unity.
> Differentiation is not yet enlightened.
> Non-differentiation is great enlightenment.

The enlightened ones, what they realize is not emptiness or substantiality. Therefore, it is neither substantiality nor emptiness. But, is enlightenment something in between substantiality and emptiness? Actually, that is not true either.

Sheng-yen Lu

2. Please Note to "Move Away From the Two Extremes"

Everybody, please remember that we, humanity, and sentient beings are bound to have beginnings and ends. To put it simply, there are births and deaths. Yet, enlightenment is neither birth nor death.

We often describe enlightenment as:

> No-birth and no-cessation
> Neither birth nor death
> Neither coming nor going
> Never came and never left

Yet, do you understand their real meaning?

Huineng, the Sixth Patriarch of Zen Buddhism in China, uttered this verse:

> Bodhi is no tree,
> Neither is bright mirror a stand.

Intrinsically there isn't a thing.
Where may dust alight?

Many people complimented the profoundness of this verse, which points out that everything is emptiness. They think it is a verse of enlightenment. But, that is wrong! Huineng's verse shows reliance on emptiness which is still not enlightened. Genuine enlightenment is away from the two extremes. Please note, one must move away from the two extremes. Later, the Sixth Patriarch Huineng gave a different answer, "Do not think of good. Do not think of evil." Ha! Now that's right.

The enlightened ones, what they realize is not emptiness or substantiality. Therefore, it is neither substantiality nor emptiness. But, is enlightenment something in between substantiality and emptiness? Actually, that is not true either.

I am a practitioner of Vajrayana teachings. If you are a Vajrayana cultivator, you will understand the Four Joys:

Joy [ananda] - Transformation (initiating transformation)
Perfect Joy [paramananda] - Progress (abiding in Great Bliss)
Joy of Cessation [viramananda] - Accomplishment (abiding in Clear Light)
Innate joy [sahajananda] - Emptiness (Perfection)

Through diligent Vajrayana cultivation, you will gradually achieve transformation, progress, accomplishment, and emptiness.

Originally, I thought the emptiness of innate joy is enlightenment. Later, I realized that the emptiness of innate joy is not really enlightenment. True enlightenment is definitely not emptiness. It is also definitely not substantiality.

Enlightenment is:

Shakyamuni Buddha holding up a flower
Zen Master Tianlong [Tenryu] holding up a finger
My "Golden Rooster standing on one leg"

My first Sutra-Buddhism teacher was the Venerable Yinshun. He was from the Sanlun School [a Chinese Madhyamaka sect], which emphasizes doctrines and philosophies. Master Yinshun was a prolific writer, and his writings on Buddhist philosophy greatly influenced the Chinese Buddhist community. Doctrines are very important and cannot be neglected. Through understanding and validating doctrines, you can identify which level you have achieved. My final Vajrayana teacher was Vajra Acharya Thubten Dargye. He was a guru who placed great importance on diligent cultivation. He felt that doctrines and diligent cultivation must be mutually complementary to achieve perfection. They are like the wheels of a car, or the two wings of a bird.

By integrating doctrines and diligent cultivation as one, I endeavored to achieve the fruition of Buddhahood and gradually achieved accomplishment. In both cultivation and doctrine, I achieved siddhi accomplishment. When I finally achieved enlightenment, I did not achieve it through doctrines or cultivation. Please note to move away from the two extremes, that is enlightenment.

Enlightened one,
It is not emptiness,
Nor is it substantiality.
So, it is neither substantiality nor emptiness.

Did the Buddha give any dharma teachings? Did the Buddha turn the dharma wheel? I will hit you on your head with a vajra if you say yes.

Sheng-yen Lu

3. The Evil of Sexual Misconduct

In the chapter "Direct Revelation," I mentioned an arrogant person who claimed to attain enlightenment. Yet, why am I certain that he has not achieved enlightenment? I know that because he claimed that Tibetan Buddhism is a faith perverted by sexual misconduct. Just on that statement alone, I am certain that he doesn't know what enlightenment is.

Let me explain to him:

In the wisdom eye of enlightened people, there is no such thing as good or evil; they do not take sides. By accusing Tibetan Buddhism of being a faith perverted by sexual misconduct, you have taken a side (exposed your flaw). You definitely aren't enlightened. You don't even know what enlightenment is. You have a long way to go. You made me laugh my socks off!

You said that in the Buddha's three turnings of the dharma wheel, the absolute truth was only revealed in the scriptures of the third turning of the dharma wheel. I want you to pay close attention to this exchange between Shakyamuni Buddha and Manjushri Bodhisattva:

When Shakyamuni Buddha was about to enter nirvana, Manjushri

Bodhisattva implored the Buddha not to leave. Manjushri pleaded, "Buddha, please stay in this world to teach the dharma. Buddha, please turn the dharma wheel once again."

The Buddha replied, "Manjushri, you have great wisdom. Even you don't realize that I have never taught any dharma nor have I turned the dharma wheel?"

Only then did Manjushri Bodhisattva regain his composure and realize the true essence of the Buddha's teachings.

Now, let me ask you: Did the Buddha give any dharma teachings? Did the Buddha turn the dharma wheel? I will hit you on your head with a vajra if you say yes. Have you lost your mind? Didn't you claim to be enlightened? You have just slandered the Buddha.

Now let's discuss your accusation that Tibetan Buddhism is a faith perverted by sexual misconduct. In the real world, besides monks, priests, and nuns who abstain from sex to uphold their vows of celibacy, every animal in this world came about as the result of carnal desire. Not just animals alone, even plants are conceived through sexual reproduction. Is sexual desire evil? If sexual desire is evil, then everyone is wicked and evil.

Your parents' sexual desire led to your birth. Can you guarantee that the sex between your parents was proper? In the eyes of ordinary people, sex is sex. What's proper or improper about it? Is sex necessarily evil? May I remind you that all sentient beings are born as result of sex.

Tibetan Buddhism transforms lust into a method of cultivation involving visualization, mantra chanting, and mudra. It teaches sentient beings that even lust can be used as a means for cultivation (the practitioners must uphold Differentiated Rules of Liberation).

Do not misinterpret this type of cultivation. It is not the perverse act that you are thinking. Do not put your mind in the gutter. Do not let your mind be deviant and evil. There are very few people who are qualified to practice this kind of cultivation anyways (they must have already achieved accomplishment in the cultivation of qi, channels, and drops).

I think that you have a filthy mind, so you claimed that Tibetan Buddhism is evil. Let me tell you, Vajrayana expands your mind to be boundless, but you don't have what it takes to cultivate Vajrayana teachings. Sorry, you really do not. You are dirty. You don't even know what innate purity is. How can you be considered enlightened?

I say, "You don't understand the meaning of 'neither pure nor impure.'"

> Through nothing to gain,
> Hence, we see through,
> Anger and greed,
> Offenses and delusion,
> This is not the opposition of self versus others.
> On the level of nothing to gain,
> Everything is equal.
> That is the genuine truth of the universe.

Vajrayana is fundamentally, without a doubt, the dharma gate to realize emptiness.

Sheng-yen Lu

4. The Secret of Enlightenment

There isn't really any secret to enlightenment. I personally believe the issue is in the degree, level, or baseline of enlightenment. If you think there is any secret, pith instruction, special methodology that your guru has intentionally concealed, hidden, or was unwilling to share with you, then you have misunderstood him. Your teacher did not reveal certain key points because you have not attained the necessary level of cultivation accomplishment. Hence, it is inappropriate for him to reveal it to you.

> The reasons are simple:
> You will not be able to handle it.
> You will be shocked.
> You may faint.
> You may feel that enlightenment is too ordinary.
> You may feel that enlightenment is too inconceivable.

If an enlightened person reveals enlightenment to someone who is not near the level of enlightenment, the recipient may be bewildered, or even suffer great harm. Hence, the teacher must wait for the student to become mature [ready] before the teacher can put on the critical "finishing touches." This may be why the so-called secret manual cannot be taught.

I have said in the past that Vajrayana Buddhism is one of the three great dharma gates [Buddhist paths] for the realization of emptiness.

A lay Buddhist practitioner named Chen Huijian criticized my statement at that time. He wrote, "Vajrayana is not a dharma gate that realizes emptiness. The so-called three dharma gates that realize emptiness are fundamentally wrong, wrong, and wrong."

I stated the three great dharma gates are Zen, Madhyamaka [the Sanlun School], and Vajrayana Buddhism.

I shall now discuss whether or not Vajrayana Buddhism is a dharma gate that realizes emptiness. Vajrayana Buddhism consists of four classes of tantra:

> Kriya Tantra (focused on substantiality).
> Charya Tantra (focused on substantiality).
> Yoga Tantra (focused on emptiness).
> Highest Yoga Tantra (focused on emptiness).

The generation stage cultivations focus on substantiality and perfection stage cultivations focus on emptiness.

Vajrayana cultivation relies on the substantiality of our own physical body to realize the emptiness of the dharmadhatu. This is without question. What is ultimately realized by Vajrayana cultivation?

> Great Bliss (is without substantiality).
> Clear Light (is without substantiality).
> Empty Nature (is without substantiality).

Dream yoga accomplishment (is without substantiality); illusory body accomplishment (is without substantiality); rainbow body accomplishment (is without substantiality); consciousness transference accomplishment (is without substantiality); samadhi accomplishment (is without substantiality).

Everyone knows that Vajrayana practices all start with visualization. The wellspring of visualization is without substantiality, the fruition of which is also without substantiality. Hence, that is the Great Perfection. Vajrayana is fundamentally, without a doubt, the dharma gate to realize emptiness.

Do you (Chen Huijian) still have anything else to say?

Yet, what is really this secret of enlightenment? "Not Buddha, not heart, and not object." Do you understand? Can you do it?

> The human world is transitory.
> Dissonant emotions are dust from this journey.
> Anything and everything,
> Are all supreme purity.
> This is the Original Appearance.

You ask me, what is enlightenment really?
I would respond that enlightenment is always there and makes no distinction.

Sheng-yen Lu

5. Limitless Vision

If enlightenment has a limit, then can it really be enlightenment? Our vision is essentially limitless. Enlightenment is not academic study, farming, tools for material gain, wealth, nor politics. In principle, enlightenment isn't anything. Yet, enlightenment is also everything.

A Zen master asked his students, "Is it better to prosper, or to wither away?" One student answered that it is better to prosper. A second student said that it is better to wither away. A third student replied that if something prospers, then let it prosper; if something withers, then let it wither away. The Zen master responded that there is innately no prospering or withering.

Generally, Zen teachings are very deep. The back-and-forth of questions and answers creates critical junctures and inspires unanticipated answers that you would have never considered or thought of. This method of teaching often gives people an enigmatical impression, and leaves the audience in bewilderment. But, this is a very good method to guide people. Now, I would like to ask everyone to reflect upon a question.

One day, I asked several vajra masters at the Seattle Temple about drilling for fire using wood. I asked where the fire came from when you drill for fire?

Did the fire come from the wood being drilled? (Wood itself is not made of fire.)

Did the fire arise from the wood drill? (The wood drill is also not made of fire.)

Did the fire arise from the hands of the person drilling for fire? (Human hands are also not made of fire.)

Did the fire come from the force of the drilling applied onto the wood? (The drilling force is also not made of fire.)

I said to those vajra masters that none of the elements are fire, they are all different, and there was no fire present. So I asked, where did this fire come from?

They were silent. I said, only an enlightened person would really know where the fire comes from.

I will hold off on answering the question for now, and let everyone try to answer this question themselves.

My hint on the answer is as follows: There are many types of electromagnetic waves in our world. These electromagnetic waves naturally surround us and are everywhere; many even exist within our bodies. But, they are formless and tasteless. We cannot detect them with our senses. Yet, they still exist even though we cannot sense them.

You ask me, what is enlightenment really?

I would respond that enlightenment is always there and makes no distinction.

Do you understand?

Have you awakened? Hurry up and tell me where does the fire come from?

6. Mercilessly Condemning Sheng-yen Lu

Some people who see themselves as true followers of Buddhism enjoy rebuking Sheng-yen Lu. Some people who are not affiliated with any religion are also fond of condemning Sheng-yen Lu as well. These self-proclaimed true followers of Buddhism have denounced me as a non-Buddhist heathen masquerading as Buddhist, a cult leader, a great mara, a demon, a monster, a religious scam artist, a womanizing fraud, etc. Ordinary people have called me a scumbag, a con-artist exploiting people's superstitions and fears, sub-human scum, a piece of shit, insane, etc.

I laugh at these disparaging remarks, and they don't bother me a bit. I just keep happily eating my food and sleeping comfortably in my bed. My heart is like the clouds, always carefree. My mind is like a river, flowing freely.

Some people say that I am a real living buddha, which doesn't bring me joy. Some people say that I am a fake living buddha, which also doesn't make me sad. Honestly, I am not as bad as they say I am. I actually have some good qualities.

I know that all human beings have upheld the five precepts in [their past lives.] This is the mandatory requirement to be reborn as a human being. There are no really perfectly virtuous people, and there are no completely evil people. Even among good people, there is no one who is always good. By the same token, there is also no one who is completely evil. Moreover, I am an enlightened person. Haha. I understand the World Honored One's secret the best. I also understand sentient beings' secret the best as well.

I am awakened. I am all sentient beings and I am also the Tathagata.

These self-proclaimed true followers of Buddhism gnashed their teeth in fury when I said that I am a buddha. When I said that I am a good friend of Shakyamuni Buddha and we are "buddy-buddy," their anger reached the zenith. They drew a line in the sand separating us, and they wanted nothing to do with me. I am really puzzled. I am a tathagata. I am the Tathagata's brother. I am innately a buddha. There is nothing wrong with any of that. This is all very reasonable.

Buddhist sutras clearly state: "Heart, Buddha, and sentient beings are all one and the same."

Regretfully, not one sentient being in this world dares to shoulder this fact.

I thoroughly understand that "Heart is the Buddha." I thoroughly understand that [true nature is] "not heart and not buddha." I thoroughly understand that [absolute reality is] "not Buddha, not heart, and not object."

I not only understand this, but I also don't conceal this. I practice this daily in my life. It is fine whether you believe me or not. I am fine either way or any other way. That is the state of my attainment.

I know the secret of sentient beings. I know the secret of the Tathagata. If you don't study with me, who else can you follow under the light of sun and moon?

"True followers of Buddhism" - just the sound of that big title is nauseating!

7. Everyone Has What It Takes

I wrote the following verse:

> Namo the buddhas of pristine innate nature,
> The genuine essence of no defilement or obscuration.
> Spread true Buddhist teachings life after life,
> Deliver beings and receive predictions of Buddhahood time after time.

This verse is a song of enlightenment. It contains dharma for ordinary daily living, and dharma to transcend the world. There is the purity of innate nature, absence of defilement and obscuration, dissemination of genuine Buddhist teachings, and deliverance of sentient beings life after life. The meaning of this verse is "having what it takes."

Shakyamuni Buddha said, "All sentient beings have what it takes. But, they cannot achieve enlightenment because of their obscuring hindrances." What are these obscuring hindrances? They are dissonant emotions, habitual tendencies, belief in the inherent existence of self, holding the belief that things are real, hindrances of worldly knowledge of differentiating what is seemingly real, and the three poisons of greed, anger, and ignorance.

When all these obscuring hindrances are completely severed, the Buddha-nature that has always been there will emerge. That is enlightenment. Buddha-nature is still there even if you don't achieve enlightenment. Buddha-nature is also there when you do achieve enlightenment (this is no gain and no loss).

Many people separate nirvana and transmigration in cyclical existence into two different entities. They say Buddha-nature is nirvana and obscuring hindrances cause transmigration in cyclical existence. They say transmigration exists because of the Six Roots, Six Defilements, and Six Consciousness. They say transmigration exists in the five aggregates of form, feeling, perception, volition, and consciousness, and it even exists in rage, jealousy, hatred, and delusion.

Yet I say, submerge these elements of obscuring hindrances into nirvana. Wise beings should remain in cyclical existence, skillfully transforming transmigration into nirvana. This kind of nirvana is the dharma of ordinary daily living and also the dharma to transcend the world.

There are three meanings in my explanation:

1. Purification.
2. Innately possessing what it takes.
3. Transmigration and nirvana are one and the same.

In Zen Buddhism, many Zen masters have triggered enlightenment in their students by summoning them to assemble for teachings. The masters stayed silent after the students convened, then disbanded the assembly. After the assembly had been dissolved, the Zen masters would call the students to assemble once again. At the very moment that students turned their heads, the Zen masters inquired, "What is it?"

Students of great capacity would then immediately achieve enlightenment after being confronted in this way.

My guidance is:

> Assembling is transmigration.
> Disbanding is nirvana.

What is it?

What is it? What is it? What is it? What is it? What is it? Do you know?

> Buddha-nature has always been there.
> When every one of the obscuring hindrances is severed,
> Buddha-nature is revealed.
> That is enlightenment.
> Even if you don't achieve enlightenment,
> Buddha-nature is still there.
> If you achieve enlightenment,
> Buddha-nature is also there.
> This is precisely no gain and no loss.

Enlightenment is:

Something that comes through guidance.
Something that comes from enticement.
A path that is established from here,
Walking perfectly.

Sheng-yen Lu

8. Let's Start It Off With a Joke

Chen Chuangfan is one of True Buddha School's dharma sisters from California. She is such a talented comedian that her audiences fall over from laughing at her jokes.

Chen once told this joke about a husband who came home one day with two bruise marks on his face. His wife asked what happened. He explained, "I was taking a bus home today, and it was very crowded. A woman was wearing a front-zip tank top, and the zipper was set very low on her chest. I kindly zipped her up, but she slapped me in return. Then, I realized that she intentionally wanted the zipper to be low. So, I pulled her front zipper back down, but she unexpectedly slapped me again.

Wife: …

Everybody laughed at this joke.

Using this joke as the subject, I want to ask a couple of questions.

Was it right to zip her up? Was it right to zip her down? Was not helping the right thing? Or was helping the right thing?

I now ask my wise students, what would you do if you were husband and saw a woman wearing a tank top with a zipper in the front set very low on her chest?

I feel this joke contains interesting points of enlightenment. These interesting points show us how to travel on the right path. Enlightenment is:

> Something that comes through guidance.
> Something that comes from enticement.
> A path that is established from here,
> Walking perfectly.

My guidance is:

If you were in his place, would it be right if you close your eyes? Would it be right if you turned your back on the woman? Or would it right to be completely unaffected by it, see through the situation regardless whether the zipper was up or down? Or, you may have other opinions and the answer is none of the previously mentioned, or there is no right answer at all.

I invite all my noble students to reflect and contemplate on this issue. In this chapter, there is purity, defilement, no purity and no defilement, and neither this nor that.

If you are an enlightened person, what is your answer? What is the perfect course of action for handling this situation?

There is a Zen koan.

A man asked Zhaozhou, "What is Zhaozhou?"

Zhaozhou replied, "East gate, west gate, south gate, and north gate." The answer to the question of this joke is concealed within this koan.

9. Great Awakening

In Vajrayana's tantras of herukas, there are many shocking passages.

One tantra scripture says that a baby's experiences during the ten months of pregnancy are equivalent to going through all ten stages of bodhisattvahood. He or she is born as a tenth stage bodhisattva. He or she is also born completely naked without any hair, just like a buddha in the form of a monk.

It is also said in the tantra scriptures, "There is a truth that no one knows which is that all sentient beings are buddhas."

It was said that after the World Honored One revealed the supreme truth, Locana Buddha, Mamaki, the White Robe Guanyin, Taras, and an infinite number of bodhisattvas all fainted from being overwhelmed with doubts. Thus, Shakyamuni Buddha further explained that all sentient beings are buddhas, whether they have been obscured by beginningless delusion or a momentary delusion arising from a thought. It is without a doubt that they will become buddhas immediately once they sever these obscurations.

The World Honored One was referring to the delusion in the desire realm, the delusion in the form realm, delusion in the formless realm, and the delusion of sravakas and pratyekabuddhas.

The World Honored One was saying that you already innately possess [Buddha-nature]; do not seek liberation outside of yourself as you can attain buddhahood in this very body.

The World Honored One said that everything in the innate nature of true suchness is everlasting joy.

I once declared to tens of thousands of my followers while I was seated on my dharma throne that I am Lian-sheng Buddha. My noble students firmly believe in me. Yet, some other Buddhists have doubts. They want to discuss the issues of [whether True Buddha School reflects] genuine Buddhist teachings or non-Buddhist heathen teachings; whether or not I am a real living buddha or fake living buddha; and whether I am a real buddha or fake buddha.

Now, I solemnly quote the World Honored One, "All sentient beings are buddhas."

I am the one who has truly awakened to the supreme truth; I am the one who has attained great awakening.

Yet, those Buddhists who focus on external appearances still have doubts. They are ones who are the typical non-Buddhists. The word "great" in reference to my great awakening is not the superlative adjective for size to indicate whether something is big or small. Here the word "great" refers to eternity.

The World Honored One regarded ultimate bliss to be Great Bliss. This Great Bliss is not the ordinary bliss of the mundane world which is generated from dualistic conditions. That kind of ordinary bliss will become stale and [unsatisfying], and will lead to insatiable desires. As all humanity seeks pleasure, desires become insatiable and unending.

Bliss and suffering are dualistic and opposing conditions. Yet, the bliss of enlightenment is the Great Bliss. This Great Bliss is not dualistic but absolute.

You should understand that I don't need liberation because I am not in bondage. I don't need skillful means because I innately am. I don't need delusion because there is innately no delusion. I am not confused because there is no confusion.

> I am Lian-sheng Buddha.
> I am in the clear light of Great Bliss.
> If you have doubts,
> Then you are the non-Buddhist.
> I don't need liberation because I am not in bondage.
> I don't need skillful means because I innately am.
> I don't need delusion because there is innately no delusion.
> I will not be confused because there is no confusion.

A person who realizes the emptiness of substantiality will not have attachment to the material world. Without attachment, there will not be any dissonant emotions. Everything is empty of substantiality. Everything is free of bondage of dissonant emotions.

Sheng-yen Lu

10. Realize the Emptiness of Substantiality

The Great Daoist sage, Zhuangzi, once while passing a cemetery, saw a woman fanning the freshly dug soil covering a grave. Zhuangzi asked, "Why are you fanning the soil covering this grave?" The woman replied, "My late husband said I may remarry once the soil covering his coffin had dried." Zhuangzi sighed and then dried the soil swiftly with magical power. The woman happily thanked him and left.

Zhuangzi told his beautiful wife about this incident when he returned home. His wife became very angry and said, "This woman is without dignity and shame, yet you still helped her!" This led to the famous story of Zhuangzi testing his wife which is also known as "Splitting Coffin."

Not long afterward, Zhuangzi faked his own death from an illness. His wife arranged for his burial. Then, Zhuangzi magically disguised himself as a young handsome scholar. The young scholar claimed to be Zhuangzi's student and came to visit Zhuangzi. After spending several days together, Zhuangzi's wife fell in love with this handsome young man. Then, the young man revealed that he was extremely ill and his illness could only be cured by consuming a human brain. Zhuangzi's wife asked, "Could Zhuangzi's brain be used to cure your disease since he just died?" The scholar said, "Yes." Zhuangzi's wife then split open Zhuangzi's coffin with an axe intending to obtain Zhuangzi's brain. After the coffin was split open, the young man vanished. Zhuangzi stood up from his coffin and sighed. This was the summary of the famous story of Zhuangzi testing his wife.

This story made me reflect that:

> My wife is not eternally mine.
> My wealth is not eternally mine.
> My children are not eternally mine.
> High social status and material fortune are not eternally mine.

Everything of the world including:

> Life is not eternally mine.
> Houses are not eternally mine.
> Lands are not eternally mine.
> Jewelries are not eternally mine.
> Cars are not eternally mine.

The wise Zhuangzi realized the emptiness of substantiality. Living Buddha Lian-sheng also realized the emptiness of substantiality.

A person who realizes the emptiness of substantiality will not have attachment to the material world. Without attachment, there will not be any dissonant emotions. Everything is empty of substantiality. Everything is free of bondage of dissonant emotions.

I laugh and smile while observing this world. I have lived a life of laughs and smiles. I am sixty-four years old (as of 2008). I am thinking of adopting the nickname, "The Laughing Old Man." This is because I have realized the inherent emptiness of substantiality. Even dissonant

emotions are empty. Isn't this the naked World Honored One?
Someone asked, "What is sudden enlightenment?"

One Zen master responded, "Realizing there's nothing to gain, severing dissonant emotions all of a sudden."

Another Zen master said, "I saw two mud buffaloes fighting with their horns locked in combat submerging into the sea. Haven't seen or heard them since."

**You would not correctly recognize that there is
no gain or loss if you don't cultivate with dedication.**

Sheng-yen Lu

11. The Personal Deity Appears

Someone asked me, "What is the enlightenment of Vajrayana Buddhism?"

I answered, "Let's divide it into two parts."

I said:

> The body is the shrine of the personal deity. The speech is the mantra of the personal deity. The mind is the visualization of the personal deity. Through the combination of these three elements and mudras, the personal deity would appear when everything has matured. These are the practices of yoga.

The second part:

> The qi enters into the central channel through the cultivation of Vase Breathing Practice. Then, one must raise the tummo fire and burn the wisdom drops. The result of the burning of wisdom drops is the opening of the five chakras, leading the Five Buddhas and Five Vajras to appear. This second stage comprises of the Tummo Fire Practice to raise the tummo fire, Yoga of Drops to burn the drops, and Non-leakage Practice to attain the Four Joys. The Four Joys are joy, great joy, exalted

joy, and innate joy. The personal deity appears in the empty space of innate joy. The personal deity may manifest in several forms [to the practitioner such as] smoke, fire, light, and the dignified appearance of a buddha's bliss body.

Someone asked me, "Seeing the manifestation of buddhas isn't considered enlightenment in Vajrayana Buddhism. Instead, one must realize the supreme truth of the Universe after seeing the buddhas. It is that which you innately possess. There is neither gains nor losses; no gain whatsoever; and no loss whatsoever. Isn't that right?"

I replied, "Yes."

The guest asked, "Then why should anyone persistently cultivate Vajrayana practices if that is the case?"

I answered, "You would not correctly recognize that there is no gain or loss if you don't cultivate with dedication."

In a previous chapter, I made the following analogy. [To drill for fire, we use] wood, a wood drill, and our hands. [We] rotate the drill to ignite the fire. The fire is not in the wood, nor in the wood drill, nor the hands, nor the drilling motion. Yet, the combination of these ingredients creates fire.

The fire symbolizes buddhas.

The fire symbolizes light.

The fire symbolizes enlightenment.

If you delve deeply into Vajrayana Buddhism, then you will understand the interrelationships between the Five Buddhas, Five elements, Five Aggregates, Five Poisons, Five Wisdoms, Five Dakinis, Five Consorts, and Five Seed Syllables. I understand very well that the mind is still the center of Vajrayana. The mind created the phenomenal universe. The mind can create and destroy. Vajrayana cultivation uses the mind until the mind itself doesn't know there's the mind. That then can be considered enlightenment.

12. Love and Hate

Those of us with wisdom eyes see through love and hate easily while countless ordinary beings embrace them [with open arms]. Love is insistence, dissonant emotions, defilement, and attachment. Yet, when love sours, it turns into its opposite emotion, hate. Hence, I say that love is hate.

Love has turned into hate countless times in this world. Hence, there are crimes of passion. When people's love turns into hate, the intensity of that hatred can become so destructive that it destroys them and the objects of their hatred.

On this matter [of love turning into hate], I advise cultivators to handle the situation with extreme care. This is because ordinary beings often misinterpret the compassion of Buddhism as love. Hence, trouble won't be far behind.

The great love expressed by bodhisattvas is compassion. This love is different from the love of ordinary beings. Yet, this compassion is easily mistaken by ordinary beings as the same as ordinary passion. This great love is the willingness to sacrifice oneself for the good of sentient beings. Life is amusing. Love can make your bones ache. Hate can make you mutilate. Passions can run deep. Hatred can last an eternity.

Someone who resents me hired a smut writer to fabricate stories about me and compiled them into a booklet. The smut writer came to see me and gave me a preview of this booklet that had plots like they were out of the movies.

He asked, "How much is this booklet worth?"

I replied, "Wujia [priceless or worthless]."

He responded, "Please pay this 'wujia' [priceless] amount." (This was extortion)

I responded, "'Wujia' [worthless] means that it isn't worth a penny. I won't give you a penny."

He said, "I will publicize this booklet."

I told him, "Do as you please."

He said, "This booklet will ruin your reputation."

I told him, "I don't have any reputation."

He didn't understand that I am an enlightened one. A person who has attained awakening knows only compassion, great love, and sacrifice. There is no such thing as fame or infamy.

Please carefully reflect on what I have said.

Without a trace of attachment, completely naked, everything is gone, emptiness of emptiness, I am actually not me.

There is no love, hate, passion, or hatred. The compassionate one is not compassionate.

A Zen master once said, "I am a donkey, ridden by ordinary beings."

13. The Immortal Vajra

The term "vajra" applies to Vajrayana dharma implements, which are the vajra and the vajra bell. Those are two of the most important dharma implements used in Vajrayana Buddhism. Vajras are made in several varieties including single-pronged, three-pronged, and five-pronged vajras. The Shingon School (Japanese Vajrayana) fashions the vajra with open prongs while Tibetan Schools prefer the vajra prongs to be closed.

The term vajra comprises of many different meanings and usages. We will not discuss all of them here. I personally feel that the vajra has three meanings: immutable, immortal, and bodhicitta. The term immutable refers to its strength, unchanging in shape, unfading in color, and eternally indestructible. The term immortal means that there is no death, not coming or going; it is everlasting. The term bodhicitta is an analogy, symbolizing the heart of a buddha, eradicating all obstacles of dissonant emotions, possessing perfect wisdom and compassion, and everything is completely perfect.

My realization is:

My life is everlasting and immortal. Your life is everlasting and immortal. Other people's lives are also everlasting and immortal.

Where was I before my birth?

My answer: "I was in deep sleep, in meditation."

Where was I after my birth?

My answer: "I awoke, emerged from meditation, and I manifested."

Where will I be after my death?

My answer: "There is no death; it is just the scenery of the original ground. There is no coming or going, no such thing as birth, no such thing as death. There isn't anything at all."

There is no sleep; there is no awaking; there is no meditation; there is no exiting meditation; there is no manifestation; and there is no non-manifestation.

There is neither birth nor death. That's the way it intrinsically is.

My first two answers are phenomena-based. The third answer is formless. My enlightenment is that of third answer.

My noble students, do you all understand?

I hear my students calling out to me:

"Grand Master Lu, you have such great compassion, please rescue us!"

"Grand Master Lu, please protect us, bestow us with good fortune, and fulfill our wishes!"

"Grand Master Lu, for the sake of sentient beings, please teach us Buddhadharma so that we can leave suffering and gain happiness. Please don't forsake anyone."

"Grand Master Lu, please demonstrate your great miraculous power to prevent disasters from happening, increase our fortune and wisdom, bless our families to stay together, and make all of our enemies retreat."

"Grand Master Lu, please take us to the Pure Land so we are free from transmigrating in the six realms of cyclic existence."

"Grand Master Lu, I vow to attain enlightenment instantly, and to attain buddhahood in this very body."

I did not do anything, I also did not not-do anything; everything is already completed.

Can everyone understand my enlightenment, the enlightenment of this immortal vajra? Can you do it?

> Sever the absolute authority,
> Then you can find the original appearance.
> You only need to clearly recognize the meaning of the word, buddha,
> Then you will not have attachment towards, nor obscurations of, buddha.
> You can experience and realize the supreme truth without any limits.
> Yet, the "self" is the supreme truth,
> Which is reaching absolute liberation.

Absolutely, attain the genuine state; be vajra-like, immutable, immortal, and bodhicitta. This kind of authenticity is incomparable and peerless.

Sheng-yen Lu

15. I Am a Non-Buddhist Heathen

I have been regarded as a non-Buddhist heathen since I was twenty-six years old. The reasons were simple: I had my divine eyes opened at age twenty-six; I visited heaven and hell; I saw that my past incarnation was Padmakumara and my pure land was the Maha Twin Lotus Ponds; I interacted with beings from spiritual worlds constantly, etc. These experiences set me apart from the Buddhist community in Taiwan, as if we were singing different tunes.

In the blink of an eye, I became extremely famous. My house was packed with visitors every day like a busy market. I saw around three hundred people daily who came seeking my guidance, help, or asking me to foretell their future. They all left saying I was so accurate and good. I helped cure many complicated and strange illnesses. I also cured countless strange illnesses caused by spirits (miracles). The entire religious community [of Taiwan] all knew about one person, and he was Sheng-yen Lu.

However, [the Chinese] Buddhist community kicked me out and branded me as a non-Buddhist heathen. This is a label that can never be removed once it has been given. Later, I formally studied

Buddhism. Then, the Buddhist community branded me as a non-Buddhist-heathen-masquerading-as-a-Buddhist.

This is the label that I was forced to wear all my life. I was regarded to be different and they treated me differently. The Buddhist community classified me as a non-Buddhist heathen - not part of authentic Buddhism. They said that I was a mutation, a mutant, and an alien. Even worse, they regarded me as a natural disaster like flood, a monster, and the devil. (I observed myself and saw that I was very genuine, not as scary as they made me out to be).

After my awakening, I negated differences. Please note the word "differences." I realized the Prajnaparamita class of Buddhist scriptures. There are no differences in Prajnaparamita. After my enlightenment, my patience and tolerance became exceptional. I became extremely carefree and relaxed, I passionately embraced the beauty of nature. I gained complete control over my own happiness and nothing really bothered me. I delivered sentient beings when the affinity presented itself. I let the good and the bad come and go as they pleased.

I wrote this verse:

> Forty years, I crisscrossed this world.
> Meeting countless people, who stay or go.
> Numbers of Dharma teachings given, never counted.
> No suffering, happiness, or cessation.

Listen to this one piece of advice from me. No matter whether something is alive or not, everything is all part of this boundless unity. Differentiation is not yet enlightened; non-differentiation is great enlightenment.

Awaken, awaken, awaken, awaken, awaken, awaken, awaken, have you awakened yet?

Forty years, I crisscrossed this world.
Meeting countless people, who stay or go.
Never counting the numbers of Dharma teachings given.
No suffering, no happiness, or cessation.

Reincarnation is the Buddha; reincarnation is the world's savior; reincarnation is exiting meditation; reincarnation is one with supreme enlightenment; and reincarnation is non-differentiation.

Sheng-yen Lu

16. The Supremely Enlightened One

I can say that I don't need to learn anymore! I can also say that I don't need to cultivate anymore! This is because I am someone who is supremely enlightened.

Anyone who hears this declaration would certainly respond that this person is insane, arrogant, and shameless! "Is this person crazy? How can this person reach the state of the Buddha? He must be a big fraud, a great charlatan, this Sheng-yen Lu! A great conman, this Sheng-yen Lu! The greatest fraud, this Sheng-yen Lu!" The people of this world will forever criticize me, even after I die, saying that the world only has one Buddha, Shakyamuni Buddha. There isn't a second Buddha, Sheng-yen Lu.

I will earnestly tell everyone: *Fahua Xuanzan* [A commentary on the *Lotus Sutra*] states, "The Three Higher Trainings are discipline, meditation, and wisdom. Diligently cultivating these trainings is called 'have learned' [saiksa]. Once these trainings are perfected, the cultivation may cease. This is called 'non-learning' [asaiksa]."

The *Fahua Jiaxiangshu* [another commentary on the *Lotus Sutra*] states, "If one studies with wholehearted devotion to find the supreme truth and practices with vigor and perseverance, then it is called 'learning.' If the heart seeking for the truth is fulfilled and there is no need to progress further, it is called 'non-learning.'"

The Path of Non-learning is one of the three paths. It is the path which severs the confusion of the Three Realms, realizes and experiences the supreme truth, attains perfect wisdom and exhausts all needs for additional learning. Non-learning really does exist.

I also want to point out that the Kagyu School's Mahamudra stages are:

1. One-pointedness Yoga
2. Simplicity Yoga
3. One-taste Yoga
4. Non-meditation Yoga

Non-cultivation [which refers to non-meditation yoga] does exist.

I will let everyone take a look at my enlightenment! My essence is the bliss of nirvana. Pay attention, everyone. Nirvana is non-learning; nirvana is non-cultivation; nirvana is meditation; nirvana is always there; nirvana is making no distinction.

Pay attention, everyone: My physical manifestation is reincarnation. Reincarnation is the Buddha; reincarnation is the world's savior; reincarnation is exiting meditation; reincarnation is one with supreme enlightenment; and reincarnation is non-differentiation.

My validation of enlightenment is: nirvana and reincarnation is one-and-the-same, reincarnation and nirvana is one-and-the-same. Nirvana is reincarnation. Reincarnation is nirvana.

That was why I said, "Non-learning is also learning. Non-cultivation is also cultivation. This is called the learning of non-learning, the cultivation of non-cultivation. I have given a very detailed explanation and everyone should reflect on it. If you still don't understand, I should hit you with a stick. You might as well stay confused forever!

You're killing me!

Dreams are the existence of non-existence. The human world is the existence of non-existence. Meditation is the existence of non-existence. The three realms are the existence of non-existence. Nirvana is the existence of non-existence. Transmigration in cyclic existence is the existence of non-existence.

Sheng-yen Lu

17. Seeing Shakyamuni Buddha

I said that I have seen Shakyamuni Buddha. I saw him teaching at the highest heaven of the form realm, the Akanistha Heaven. I saw him in a tuxedo strolling through a street. I saw him drinking coffee in a coffee shop waiting for someone. That someone was me. I joined him to drink coffee. Then, Shakyamuni Buddha used a pen to write down the name, "Great Light Unhindered Buddha," as my title. I responded, "The word 'great' is too big. I'm afraid to use it." The Buddha laughed and wrote the down the word, "lotus." I accepted it. Hence, I am Lotus Light Unhindered Buddha.

Many people ridiculed me after I shared this story.

One Vajrayana rinpoche said that Shakyamuni Buddha had been dead for over two thousand six hundred, Sheng-yen Lu must have seen a ghost!

A Sutra School reverend said, "Nobody believes the stuff that mad man, Sheng-yen Lu, has to say."

There was one part of the story that I was too afraid to share because it would bring about even more ridicule. After we talked for a while, the Buddha told me that he had to use the restroom and rushed off.

When he returned, he said, "I was holding in my pee and feel much better now." Then the Buddha and I talked animatedly and joyfully about the assembly on the Vulture Peak Mountain.

A prominent and senior monk once asked me privately about this story. He asked, "Is it true?" I told him, "Decide for yourself." He said, "This isn't something to joke about." In a very serious tone, I responded, "I wouldn't dare to joke about the founder of Buddhism." The senior monk still shook his head, not really believing my story.

As a man with wisdom eyes, I say an object that exists is merely a state.

Dreams are the existence of non-existence. The human world is the existence of non-existence. Meditation is the existence of non-existence. The three realms are the existence of non-existence. Nirvana is the existence of non-existence. Transmigration in cyclic existence is the existence of non-existence.

Only those with this kind of awakening can see Shakyamuni Buddha. Only those with this kind of enlightenment can say that there is no delusion, no birth, and no cessation.

Even if the author of that book, "Real and Fake Living Buddha," and his teacher wanted to be my attendants, I wouldn't take them. They can wipe my butt. Hehe. Haha.

18. Nagarjuna is a Good Chap

I say that Nagarjuna Bodhisattva is a good chap. This isn't belittling him but praising him. Calling him a good chap is the most affectionate, appropriate, and suitable praise. If Nagarjuna saw me, I would be delighted if he jokingly said "Sheng-yen Lu, you dumb kid." This is how old friends who go back a long way greet each other. Sometimes when a person in his eighties or nineties sees an old friend, he would say something along the lines of, "Hey, old man Huang, you ain't dead yet!" Then, the friend may respond, "Ah, Lin you old geezer, you aren't dead either." That's the way two old friends joyfully greet each other. For me to call Nagarjuna a good chap and for him to call me a dumb kid are all expressions of affection.

Nagarjuna was born in Southern India seven hundred years after Shakyamuni Buddha entered nirvana. He was a student of Asvaghosa's student, Kapimala. Nagarjuna was the teacher of Kanadeva [Kanadeva is also known as Aryadeva].

Nagarjuna studied the *Avatamsaka Sutra* while he visited the naga's palace. Then, he opened the iron tower and disseminated the Vajrayana teachings. Eight Vajrayana and Sutra Schools traced their lineages to him as the founder of their traditions. Nagarjuna was the reincarnation of the Sublime Cloud, King of Liberation Tathagata, Asvaghosa was the reincarnation of Radiance of Sun, Moon, and Star Buddha, and I, old man Lu, am the Lotus Light Unhindered Buddha.

Nagarjuna stayed in the naga's palace for ninety days to read through the Buddhist scriptures preserved by the nagas. The volume of scriptures he read was ten times that of the Buddhist scriptures preserved in the human realm. Nagarjuna's Madhyamaka and Maitreya's Yogacara [Mind-Only] teachings are the two centers of Mahayana Buddhism. Madhyamaka teaches the principle that all phenomena are transitory, empty of inherent existence, and illusory like mirages. Yogacara teaches the principle that all phenomena are the products of consciousnesses and they exist only in the consciousness and are empty outside of it.

I admire Nagarjuna's Madhyamaka teachings. He wrote the *Mulamadhyamakakarika* [*Fundamental Treatise on the Middle Way*], *Dvadasanikaya-sastra* [*Discussion (Of Voidness) under Twelve Headings*], *Maha Prajnaparamita-sastra* [*Treatise on the Great Perfection of Wisdom*], etc.

Nagarjuna believed that to reach awakening, one must negate again and again. Negate all arguments to the very end, and at the ultimate point, enlightenment is revealed.

The *Maha Prajnaparamita-sastra* is a commentary on the *Maha Prajnaparamita-sutra* which spans six hundred scrolls. [In the *Maha Prajnaparamita-sastra*], Nagarjuna utilized the Madhyamaka philosophy for the sake of enlightening ordinary beings, enabling them to comprehend what is enlightenment. Hence, the *Maha Prajnaparamita-sastra* is monumental and Madhyamaka is the way to teach ordinary beings. I praise Nagarjuna for being a good chap because he provided a stairway for ordinary beings to directly reach enlightenment.

Someone asked me, "Sheng-yen Lu, did you use Madhyamaka or

Yogacara teachings to achieve enlightenment?"

I replied, "I didn't use eyes, ears, or mouth. Madhyamaka and Yogacara? I don't know either of them."

Then the person asked, "Then how are you a Buddha?"

I answered, "I grab air with my hands."

I wonder if everyone can do what I meant by "grab air with my hands"?

> Sufferings are a bubble, shadow, illusion, and dream;
> Happiness is also a bubble, shadow, illusion, and dream.
> No suffering and no happiness,
> Is the great happiness of liberation.

I say that there was no suffering or frustration. Why is that? Everything is like a dream, illusion, bubble, and shadow.

Sheng-yen Lu

19. Shakyamuni Buddha's Dismissal of "Challenges"

If you reflect on Shakyamuni Buddha's life after his enlightenment, you would find that it was not smooth sailing. There were many challenges and adversities. Here are some of the notable ones.

The Sundari Incident - The woman Sundari, dressed in seductive attire, claimed to have a physical relationship with the Buddha and many members of the Sangha. Later, she was murdered [by people who plotted to harm the Buddha's reputation], and her body was dumped in the trash near the Jetavana Monastery [the Buddha's retreat; as part of the plot to frame the Buddha].

The Cincamanavika Incident – Cincamanavika claimed to have been impregnated by the Buddha. She was exposed to have faked her pregnancy and was sent by detractors to defame the Buddha.

The Srigupta Incident – Srigupta invited Shakyamuni Buddha to a banquet, but Srigupta secretly plotted to murder the Buddha with poisoned food and a fire pit. Fortunately, the Buddha neutralized these threats with miraculous powers.

A Brahman, who was misled by his wife, tried to slash the Buddha with a sword and was subdued by the Buddha's miraculous powers.

Devadatta's Betrayal - Buddha's cousin, Devadatta, betrayed the Buddha. He conspired with King Ajatasatru to slay the Buddha. Devadatta's plots included releasing a drunken elephant to stomp the Buddha to death, pushing over a boulder to crush the Buddha, hiding poisonous powders in his fingernails to kill the Buddha, etc.

Devadatta also arranged for five hundred archers to ambush the Buddha. The Buddha magically transformed their arrows into flowers, thus neutralizing the threat.

In the city of Sravasti, a white dog barked at the Buddha whenever it saw the Buddha, which resulted in the revelation of the past karma of the dog.

Some say the Buddha faced ten major adversities in his life. Any ordinary person would have died from the stress of dealing with all these problems. Fortunately, the Buddha's great wisdom and miraculous powers enabled him to counteract them one by one.

Then, there was the Mara King who made all kinds of attempts to rush Shakyamuni Buddha into nirvana.

Reflecting upon on all these hardships, didn't Shakyamuni Buddha endure great stress and face incredible hardships, especially the scandals of Sundari and Cincamanavika? How many people lost their faith in the teachings because of these scandals?

The treacherous Devadatta led five hundred disciples away from the Buddha, causing an untold number of people to lose their faith as well.

When the Buddha taught the *Lotus Sutra*, five hundred monks walked out of the assembly without listening to the teachings. How much did that hurt the Buddha's heart?

Then, there were six non-Buddhist masters who constantly plotted to harm the Buddha. The Buddha had to continually deal with their persecutions. The level of suffering must have been unimaginable.

During Buddha's time, there was also a master called Mahaveer who transmited Jainism teachings. Students of Shakyamuni Buddha and Mahaveer tried to convert each other. Some students also kept going back and forth between Shakyamuni Buddha and Mahaveer. Wasn't that discouraging for the Buddha?

With the religious landscape being dominated by Hinduism during his days, wasn't the Buddha subjected to frustration and suffering?

I say that there was no suffering or frustration. Why is that? Everything is like a dream, illusion, bubble, and shadow. The Buddha dismissed all the stresses and sufferings with none other than the phrase, [everything is just a] dream, illusion, bubble, and shadow.

My heart is like the clouds, always carefree.
My mind is like a river, flowing freely.

After I embarked on the path of liberation, I discovered that the ego is the beginning of hardships and suffering. The more that I wanted to escape from these hardships and suffering, the more they clung on to me.

Sheng-yen Lu

20. I am the Merriest of Them All

We know that the Buddha faced many stressful and challenging situations during his time in the human realm. Strangely, when reflecting on my own life, I find that I have experienced many similar circumstances encountered by the Buddha, such as being falsely accused and defamed by women, persecuted by gangsters and criminals, targeted for extortion and intimidation, betrayed by students, thrust into the center of many controversies, etc. Since I was twenty-six years old until today, at sixty-four years of age, the criticisms and slanders have never stopped. These critiques come in all forms such as word-of-mouth, commentaries, news articles, TV reports, internet postings, magazine articles, books, etc. Were they positive and constructive? They surely weren't! Were they all negative in nature? Most certainly.

Outsiders say that Living Buddha Lian-sheng is a very controversial figure. This is an accurate observation without any embellishment. After I embarked on the path of liberation, I discovered that the ego is the beginning of hardships and suffering. The more that I wanted to escape from these hardships and suffering, the more they clung on to me. I really felt great torment. It was agony, agony, and more agony; suffering upon suffering; endless hardships; the greatest pain; the worst agony.

I have said in the past that it wouldn't be enough even if I committed suicide one hundred times. Luckily, I seem to be very resilient. Also, a benefactor would always come to my rescue whenever the suffering and the hardships were on the brink of overwhelming me. This rescuer was none other than the Golden Mother of Jade Pond. Later, I saw through these hardships. I became awakened and attained the eyes of wisdom. Agony, agony, and more agony became happiness, happiness, and more happiness. The suffering upon suffering became happiness upon happiness. The endless hardships became endless happiness. The greatest pain became the greatest joy. The worst agony became supreme happiness.

I became the merriest of them all. I have fully grasped the essence of Shakyamuni Buddha's four word teaching of dream, illusion, bubble, and shadow. The essence of these four words can overcome all [obstacles]. Suffering is merely a dream, illusion, bubble, and shadow. Happiness is also merely a dream, illusion, bubble, and shadow. No suffering and no happiness is the most joyous carefree liberation.

I invite noble students to reflect on the following exchange.

Someone asked me, "What is your family name?" I answered, "I did not receive a family name."

Then, he asked, "What is your [personal] name?" I responded, "I didn't receive a [personal] name."

Then, he asked, "Who are you?" I responded, "A dream, illusion, bubble, and shadow."

He asked, "Haven't you accomplished anything?" I answered, "Accomplishments are also just dreams, illusions, bubbles, and shadows."

(Noble students, do you understand yet? "Oh heavens, Oh heavens!")

21. The Constantly Changing Sheng-yen Lu

There have been people who have made the criticism that Sheng-yen Lu has a propensity for change and is good at changing. They derided Sheng-yen Lu as being difficult to figure out and someone who is intentionally creating an aura of mystery around himself. They claimed that the words of Sheng-yen Lu were non-definitive and constantly shifting.

A critic said that Sheng-yen Lu was a follower of Christianity, who moved on to Daoism, Sutra Buddhism, and Vajrayana Buddhism. Sheng-yen Lu claimed to be Vairocana Buddha, then he claimed to be Locana Buddha, Amitabha Buddha, Padmakumara, and Living Buddha Lian-sheng. Sheng-yen Lu was also Sariputra, Magnificent Lion Buddha, Master Kukai, Lotus Light Unhindered Buddha, Liansheng Buddha, etc. Now, Sheng-yen Lu is not just the Great Blessing Vajra, but he is also Hevajra, Cakrasamvara, Yamantaka, Guhyasamaja, and Kalachakra. Sheng-yen Lu also claimed that he attained enlightenment. Who knows what the heck this enlightenment is?

I will respond to the main thrust of these criticisms using

Shakyamuni Buddha as an example. Shakyamuni Buddha has three bodies: his truth body is Mahavairocana Buddha; his bliss body is Buddha Locana; and his emanation body is Shakyamuni Buddha.

If we read Shakyamuni Buddha's Jataka Tales, we will learn that Shakyamuni Buddha had been a renunciant sage, the Himalaya Kumara, a king of elephants, a king of deer, a king of the monkeys, and a king of the eagles, and countless other incarnations in his past lives.

Shakyamuni Buddha sought teachings from over twenty thousand teachers [in his past lives]; thus the number of his incarnations is beyond elaboration. Shakyamuni Buddha taught eighty-four thousand antidotes to remedy eighty-four thousand afflictions of sentient beings. The numbers of his teachings are unmatched by anyone in the world.

Once, while in meditation, Shakyamuni transformed into Kalachakra and taught the Kalachakra Tantra to King Suchandra. On another occasion, Shakyamuni Buddha transformed into Ucchusma to pacify the Conch-shell Hair Lord of Heaven, etc. Shakyamuni Buddha's examples show conclusively that these myriad transformations are all just Shakyamuni Buddha.

This is:

> Nothing on heaven or earth is comparable to the Buddha.
> Peerless even in all the worlds of the ten directions.
>
> Of all things that I have seen and encountered,
> Not one of them is comparable to the Buddha.

Shakyamuni Buddha is the teacher of the three realms, the compassionate father of beings from four forms of birth, the guide for humans and gods, and emanation of three types of transformation body.

I will also give an example of Avalokitesvara's transformation:

> Appearing in thirty-two transformations throughout the cosmos,
> Rescuing and delivering beings for millions of millions of eons.
> The sweet nectars in her vase are often sprinkled,
> [Using a] willow branch which has gone through countless seasons in her hand.
> Pray to her from myriad places, and she shall appear.
> The ferry boat eternally delivering people from the sea of suffering.

The thirty-two transformations of Avalokitesvara are quite well known. Then, there is the multitude of her transformations recorded in "Universal Gateway Chapter" [of the *Lotus Sutra*]. She appears in the most suitable transformation to deliver those in need.

I have attained the accomplishment of meditating in samadhi in one place and appearing elsewhere (meditation accomplishment) and generating millions of emanations (illusory body accomplishment).

> Within equality of all Dharma, I have already merged with all sentient beings.
> All sentient beings also live within me as well.
> The hindrances of dissonant emotions and knowledge are both nonexistent.
> This is the Wisdom of Equality in Nature.

Even if you gratified all of your desires and obtained all of the material possessions you desire, the resulting reality would still be empty (the Nature of Emptiness).

Sheng-yen Lu

22. Desire, Desire, Desire, Desire, Desire

A student asked me, "Does an enlightened one still have desires?" I answered, "Yes."

The student then asked, "When the desires are not fulfilled, wouldn't it become dissonant emotions?"

I answered, "Yes, unfulfilled desires would become dissonant emotions."

This student continued, "Then, should one eliminate desires? Or should one gratify them?"

I said, "One should neither eliminate nor gratify desires."

The student responded, "I don't understand."

I replied, "I understand even less."

The student had a completely baffled look on his face.

My guidance is: Monastic Buddhists of the both of past and present aim to eliminate desires by devoting themselves to austerity. Advanced practitioners of austerity eliminate their desires for passions and material possessions by maintaining a very bland lifestyle. They wear monastic robes, carry begging bowls, and live in seclusion. Some say "Desires are rampant like weeds. Suppress them with a large boulder, and the weeds will stop growing." But, as soon as the boulder is removed, the weeds will sprout back to life.

If someone lives to gratify his desires and is adrift in the sea of desire, this is also not right. Isn't that the life which ordinary people seek? Chasing after fame, fortune, sexual gratification, and fulfillment of desires, these are completely contrary to the lives of spiritual cultivators. If a person lives to fulfill his desires, then he becomes seedier than ordinary people. How can anyone transcend the suffering of this world?

My enlightenment is:

Desire is emptiness. Fame and social-standing are emptiness. Gold, silver, and jewelry are emptiness. Sexual desire is emptiness. Indulging in desire is emptiness. Even if you gratified all of your desires and obtained all of the material possessions you desire, the resulting reality would still be empty (the Nature of Emptiness).

The Householder Vimalakirti of the *Vimalakirti Sutra* is the embodiment of a cultivator who neither eliminated desires nor gratified them. This great householder demonstrated that desires are also Buddhadharma. Desires which are not desires are desires. Dissonant emotions that are not dissonant emotions are dissonant emotions. Dissonant emotions are Bodhi.

The Householder Vimalakirti was an enlightened being who neither denied nor gratified desires. He was not constrained to rules or rituals, but his spiritual achievements far exceeded those of ascetic monks who dedicated their lives to austerity.

One of the monks who I ordained came to see me.

I asked him, "Where do you want to go?"

He answered, "I want to receive the threefold platform of precepts."

I asked him, "What are the benefits for receiving the threefold platform of precepts?"

He responded, "It releases one from the cycle of life and death."

I said, "There is a person, who did not receive the threefold platform of precepts, but he is also free from the sufferings of life and death. Do

you know who he is?"
    The monk was stunned.
    (I ask, my noble students, do you know the answer?)

Vajrayana is attaining the three secrets of the tathagatas through the cultivation of the three secrets of body, speech, and mind.

Sheng-yen Lu

23. There Is No Hinayana, Mahayana, or Vajrayana Vehicle

I declare that "there is innately no Hinayana, Mahayana, or Vajrayana Vehicle." This statement probably would startle many members of the Buddhist community, believing that I am subverting Buddhism.

In Buddhism, the Hinayana Vehicle focuses on individual salvation through one's own cultivation efforts. The cultivators aspire to achieve realization of the true suchness and reach the shore of liberation. This is to say, achieve fruition through one's own effort, and the highest attainable stage is arahathood. Currently, Hinayana Buddhism is prevalent in Southeastern Asian countries like Thailand, Myanmar, Laos, and Cambodia.

In contrast, the Mahayana Vehicle focuses on universal salvation of attaining enlightenment to help others to attain enlightenment. In addition, the cultivators must completely devote themselves to the welfare of others, even at the expense of sacrificing themselves to help others achieve enlightenment. The cultivators are to ferry others to the shore of liberation first before stepping onto the shore themselves. The cultivators are to put the interests of sentient beings before their own; that's the spirit of the Mahayana Vehicle, the spirit of the bodhisattvas. Mahayana Buddhism is prevalent in countries such as China, Korea, and Japan.

Vajrayana Buddhism was the final form of Buddhism that was prevalent in India, and it is considered to be part of Mahayana Buddhism. Vajrayana is attaining the three secrets of the tathagatas through the cultivation of the three secrets of body, speech, and mind. It also uses the cultivation of qi, channels and drops to merge mind and qi as one, and realizes the innate bliss and the innate wisdom of Buddha wisdom. It uses the fastest method to attain accomplishment and buddhahood in the present body. The Vajrayana teachings transmitted in Tibet is called Tibetan Buddhism. The Vajrayana teachings prevalent in China during the Tang Dynasty are called Zhenyan Buddhism. The Vajrayana teachings prevalent in Japan are called Shingon Buddhism.

Those are the three major types of Buddhism, and the word "vehicle" means a cart or wagon.

There is another interpretation:

Hinayana cultivates the practice of emptiness, through hearing the teachings the Tathagata gave in this world, realizing the Four Noble Truths, and attaining arhathood. The Middle Vehicle cultivates the practice of emptiness, realizes the Twelve Links of Dependent Origination by his own observation of the external phenomenal world, and attains pratyeka-buddhahood. Mahayana [the Great Vehicle] cultivates the Six Paramitas, plants the causes for the thirty-two marks of nobility, and attains the supreme bodhi.

Yet, after my enlightenment, I say, "The three vehicles don't exist at all; there isn't even one vehicle. There are no Four Noble Truths, Twelve Links of Dependent Origination, or Six Paramitas. There isn't anything at all."

Does anyone understand my enlightenment?

A student sought to be ordained as a monk. I said to him, "I don't have anything. Why are you coming here to join the monastic order?"

He said, "To undergo the training of discipline, meditation, and wisdom."

I replied, "I don't have disciple, meditation or wisdom here."

He was thoroughly puzzled.

My hint to everyone is that discipline, meditation, and wisdom are the three higher trainings; it is part of the process of studying and practicing the Buddhadharma. Yet, for those who have attained Buddha wisdom, perfect enlightenment, and for those with realization, what need do they have for discipline, meditation, and wisdom? "The clouds are in the blue sky; the water is in the bottle." Do you understand? Do you really understand?

> The three vehicles don't exist at all, there isn't even one vehicle.
> There are no Four Noble Truths,
> The Twelve Links of Dependent Origination,
> nor the Six Paramitas.
> There isn't anything at all.

Tibetans are worried, and many people of the world share the same sentiment. This is all pretty normal. Yet, all these matters have nothing to do with whether or not the Dalai Lama is enlightened? Not a bit.

Sheng-yen Lu

24. Is the Dalai Lama Enlightened?

One of my students came to see me from Dharamasala, India. He was originally a student of the Seventeenth Karmapa (Ogyen Trinley Dorje). Later, he became my student as well. He is a white, western, Vajrayana Buddhist practitioner who also feels that he was a lama in his past life. He met the Dalai Lama in person several times.

He came to the Seattle Leizang Temple and asked me, "Is the Dalai Lama enlightened?"

I smiled and replied, "What are your thoughts on the matter?"

He said, "The Dalai Lama has been very concerned over the issue of his succession recently. He has been pondering on how the Fifteenth Dalai Lama would be selected."

There are three proposals:

1. The Tibetan people will hold a referendum to elect the Fifteenth Dalai Lama.
2. The Fifteenth Dalai Lama will be reborn elsewhere in the world instead of Tibet.
3. While he is still alive, the Fourteenth Dalai Lama will

designate an eminent lama as the Fifteenth Dalai Lama.

Also, the Dalai Lama is considering ending this line of reincarnation and not reincarnating into this world again. The Dalai Lama even mentioned the possibility of two Dalai Lamas in the future, one real and one fake.

This dilemma faced by the Dalai Lama has been reported in various publications and media outlets, creating quite a stir. This is a hot topic with many people expressing their opinions on the matter. I read this news and found it very interesting, laughable, and amusing. Of course, the reincarnation of the Dalai Lama has been an important line of succession, the most important line of reincarnation in Tibet. Many people of the world are truly concern over where this line of succession is headed.

As for Tibetans, the succession of the Dalai Lama is a religious tradition which is facing a challenge to its continuation. This line of succession was based a set of principles that evolved into a structural institution with unique characteristics. Now, the characteristics might change, so how would Tibetans adapt to it? This is a concern of the Dalai Lama, and it has troubled him for a long time. Tibetans are worried, and many people of the world share the same sentiment. This is all pretty normal. Yet, all these matters have nothing to do with whether or not the Dalai Lama is enlightened? Not a bit.

I once sat alone in a room.

A student inquired, "Why is Grand Master sitting alone?"

I replied, "No particular reason."

The student asked, "If there is no particular reason, why sit alone?"

I said, "Tranquil Dharma body, neither coming nor going."

If the Dalai Lama sees this article, I wonder if he would comprehend.

Tranquil dharma body,
Neither coming nor going.

25. Is Master Hsing Yun Enlightened?

M aster Hsing Yun can be described as a marvelous flower of the [Chinese] Buddhist community. He can truly be described as big.

I feel that his physical stature is big, his Fo Guang Shan Monastery is big, and his Buddha's Light International Association is so big that it spans around the global. His temples are numerous and big. The number of his followers is big. [His organization] is a big amalgam of eight different sects of Chinese Buddhism. Its wealth is big. Its fame is big. The large Buddha statue and stupas of Fo Guang Shan Monastery are big as well.

To be honest, all these big qualities also include the big number of its publications and the big amount of historical artifacts they have amassed. Master Hsing Yun's age and credentials are big as well. Big, big, big, big, big, big! Master Hsing Yun can be considered to be the pope of Buddhist communities similar to the Pope of the Catholic Church.

Examining the recent history of Buddhist communities, if we use physical stature as the sole basis of measurement, the leaders of three other major Buddhist orders in Taiwan: Ven. Master Sheng Yen of

Dharma Drum Mountain; Ven. Master Wei Chueh of Chung Tai Chan Monastery; and Master Cheng Yen of the Tzu Chi Foundation, are all no comparison to Master Hsing Yun.

Taking other areas into consideration, Master Hsing Yun is also worthy of being big! Yet, do these "big" qualities prove that Master Hsing Yun is enlightened? In reality, these "big" qualities have nothing to do with enlightenment. Not one bit.

A PhD degree doesn't have anything to do with enlightenment! The architectural marvel of Chung Tai Chan Monastery also doesn't have anything to do with enlightenment! Even if the Tzu Chi Foundation were to be even more charitable, it would have nothing to do with enlightenment! This also means that Master Hsing Yun's "big" qualities have nothing to do with enlightenment at all.

A person came to ask me, "Has Master Hsing Yun achieved enlightenment?"

I smiled and did not answer the question.

He continued, "Master Hsing Yun has spent his entire life in the Buddhist community from his youth to today. Has he attained enlightenment?"

I answered, "You should ask him, not me."

My guidance is as follows:

A novice monk asked me, "What kind of person is enlightened?"

I answered, "What kind of person is what kind of person? What is a person?"

The monk thought for a while and replied, "A person is a composition of [the elements of] earth, water, fire, and wind."

I retorted, "Then, what are earth, water, fire, and wind?"

The monk responded, "Then, there is no difference between people?"

I asked him, "Who told you that?"

If you can figure out, "Who told you that," if you fully realize this essence, then that is enlightenment. I don't know if Master Hsing Yun has realized this or not. Who is the one who told you that?

Family and wife, I completely let them go a long time ago.

Sheng-yen Lu

26. Vajra Master Lianxiang and Me

Vajra Master Lianxiang was my wife before I became a monk. She and I shared the same last name, and her maiden name was Li-Hsiang Lu. We also had a son and daughter before I became a monk. Our son, Fo-Chi Lu, is the owner of a car shop (president). Our daughter, Fo-Ching Lu, is a Juris Doctor (lawyer).

Whenever people in the religious community criticize me, they often start with the charge that Grand Master Lu has a wife and children. They would say, "This is strange. How could he have a wife and children? How could a monk have a wife and children?" I keep reiterating that we were married and had children before I became a monk. I also said that the founder of Buddhism, Shakyamuni Buddha [Siddhartha Gautama], also had a wife and a son before he became a monk. Siddhartha's wife was Yasodhara, and his son was Rahula. Siddhartha not only had a wife, he also had concubines. But, Siddhartha Gautama left his householder life to cultivate. I also became a monk and went to seek the ultimate truth. Ms. Li-Hsiang Lu followed me onto this path of Vajrayana cultivation. The only thing she does for me today is cook. The only thing I do for her today is teach her the Buddha-dharma.

We don't share the same bed or bedroom. We don't even hug each other. If we were still a married couple, that would be truly tragic. I will give a simple overview of my relationship with Master Lianxiang. Between us, there is no love (the love of ordinary people). There is no hate (the hatred of ordinary people). We are not friends (friends in the ordinary world). We are not enemies (enemies of the ordinary world). There isn't anything between us. I am not the master, and she is not the servant. We are just two spiritual cultivators. I am Living Buddha Lian-sheng. She is Vajra Master Lianxiang.

I reflected on what leaving the householder life really means. Do you have to go the extreme east while your family moves to the extreme west? Or do you need to go to the extreme north, leaving your family behind in the extreme south? Do you have to be forever separated from your family to have truly left your householder life? To be honest, there is nothing between us. Genuinely, there is nothing between us. Our relationship is like water, bland water. Given that, do we still need to be separated by distance? [My dedication to the Buddhist teachings is such that] I would climb to stand on the highest mountain peak. [My perseverance to stay on this path is such that] I would trudge on the floor of the deepest ocean. Family and wife, I completely let them go a long time ago.

While seated on the dharma throne, I once asked, "We don't have love or hate. We are not friends or enemies. What is this?"

The students were puzzled.

I asked, "What is this?"

If there are noble students who can decipher the insight to this question, how can they not realize the supreme truth!

> Having passed through thousands of foamy waves together in this bustling world,
> Just companions travelling on this Vajrayana path today.

27. Criticism of Vajrayana

There are lots of modern Buddhist practitioners today criticizing Vajrayana. One Yogacara ["Mind-only"] school practitioner charged, "Tibetan Buddhism is a faith perverted by sexual obscenity." Others mocked: "Vajrayana Buddhism is a monster bred from the fusion of Brahmanism and Hinduism." "Shakyamuni Buddha only taught what is contained in the earliest form of Buddhism. Vajrayana Buddhism permits gods to be part of Buddhism which is contrary to Shakyamuni Buddha's teachings." "Do not conduct fire homas. The fire homa offering is a religious ritual of Brahmanism and Hinduism, forbidden by Shakyamuni Buddha." "The mantras found in Buddhist sutras were added by other people during later eras." "We have to abide by the teachings of Shakyamuni Buddha, and the Buddha only taught what is found in the earliest form of Buddhism." After the Buddha entered nirvana, Mahayana Buddhism attained ascension.

Later, it was the ascension of Vajrayana Buddhism. This marked the gradual corruption of the Buddha-dharma. Vajrayana Buddhism began to flourish about five hundred to one thousand years after the Buddha's nirvana. This is the Age of Dharma Degeneration and Extinction. "Vajrayana Buddhism's ascension signified the destruction of Buddhism. Vajrayana Buddhism is a corrupted faith that is not true Buddhism." "Vajrayana is really a heathen faith."

The followers of the earliest form of Buddhism, the Hinayana Buddhist monks, firmly believe that Shakyamuni Buddha only taught the earliest form of Buddhism. Only the cultivation methods used by Sariputra, Mahamaudgalyayana, Mahakasyapa, Ananda, and other [direct disciples of the Shakyamuni Buddha] are genuine Buddhist practices. They believe that the Mahayana scriptures are forgeries. Others say that Vajrayana teachings are the fusion of Brahmanism and Hinduism. These types of arguments are very persuasive to Buddhist followers, as if Shakyamuni Buddha only taught the earliest form of Buddhism.

In reality, Shakyamuni Buddha embedded Mahayana philosophies in the Hinayana scriptures and codes of discipline, and only Mahayana philosophies can fully express the essence of Buddhism.

Furthermore, Buddhist teachings never cast away Brahma. Lord Buddha also understood the need to be inclusive toward Brahmanism and Hinduism. Vajrayana Buddhism emerged with the inclusion of folk beliefs [of India] which facilitated greater acceptance of the Buddhist teachings by the general populace. Vajrayana Buddhism conveys the essence of Buddhist teachings in stages by being inclusive (generation stage) [in the introductory phase], and then pristine (perfection stage) [in the advance phase]. Buddhism's demise in India was caused by Islamic invasions, and not caused by the ascension of Vajrayana Buddhism.

What does all of this have anything to do with enlightenment?

I say that they are related.

Someone asked me, "[When Master] Danxia burnt wooden buddha statues, did buddhas get burned?"

I replied, "The buddhas weren't burnt."

The person then asked, "When the offerings were burnt in fire homas, did buddhas come to receive the offerings?"

I answered, "The buddhas did not consume the offerings."

The person pressed, "If buddhas don't consume the offerings, then why should people conduct fire homa offerings?"

I countered, "Do you eat every day? Do you burn incense and make water offerings [every day]?"

The person fell silent.

Let me ask you, "What did you realize from this simple series of questions?"

> A person who realizes the emptiness of substantiality,
> Would not be attached to the phenomenal world.
> Without attachment, there would not be any dissonant emotions.
> Everything is empty of substantiality.
> Everything is free from the bondage of dissonant emotions.

All that you can attain is emptiness; all the accomplishments are emptiness. All the honors are emptiness. Everything that you think you can cling onto is all emptiness, all is emptiness.

Sheng-yen Lu

28. How Much Time Is Left in This Life?

There was a rhyme that laments studying geometry back in my school days.
It went like this:

> Time left in this life, how much ?
> Learn geometry, how much more?
> Don't learn geometry, how much less?
> How much time is left in this life?
> Life, how much time is left?

In retrospect, this rhyme lamenting studying geometry actually contains some profound truths of life.

In the span of a hundred years , what do you really capture? What do you really accomplish? What honor do you really achieve? What do you really attain? If you win a Nobel Prize, Academy Award for Motion Picture, Olympic Gold Medal, Top Prize for Innovation, Most Valuable Player, or are listed as one of the wealthiest people in the world, you should be at the top of your field and world famous. But, after a hundred years, what do you really gain if you won? If you didn't win, what do you really lose?

Have you thought about the real value of these awards? What value do these awards add to your life? What do these achievements fulfill? For example, Yang Chuan-kwang was an Olympic Silver Medalist for Decathlon. What good did this silver medal do for him in his life? What good does it do for him after his death? How long does the honor and fame last? Gradually, it all fades away. Who will remember him? I sighed, "Oh heavens, Oh heavens!"

All these examples can be summed up with one unflinchingly direct Buddhist saying - "for a time." Between one hundred years before the beginning of the Common Era and the second century of Common Era, the Mahayana prajna series of scriptures were recorded. The main topic of these scriptures is the subject of emptiness. Don't you think so? The hundred year life span is emptiness, and so are all the awards. All that you can attain is emptiness; all the accomplishments are emptiness. All the honors are emptiness. Everything that you think you can cling onto is all emptiness, all is emptiness.

Some people may quickly jump to conclusions and assume that Sheng-yen Lu's enlightenment must be the realization of emptiness. Emptiness must be enlightenment.

I said, "That's not it."

I will explain further. Someone brought a picture of me, and said, "This is Sheng-yen Lu."

I asked him, "If the guy in the picture is Sheng-yen Lu, then who am I?"

He said, "One and the same."

I asked, "So if I die, is the picture Sheng-yen Lu?"

The person didn't know how to answer my question.

Please reflect on this question, "Is the picture Sheng-yen Lu?" (Who is Sheng-yen Lu? Who is Sheng-yen Lu?)

29. The Buddhas of the Seventeenth Stage

I guarantee that this topic will cause a great uproar and commotion in the Buddhist community once it is out. They will declare that "Sheng-yen Lu has lost his mind and gone crazy!!!" "Sheng-yen Lu is subverting Buddha-dharma. He has a lot of nerve. No one else in this world has got more nerve than he does." "What kind of stunt is Sheng-yen Lu pulling?" "How can you go higher than the highest?" "This is just bullshit!" "Don't believe him!"

Those who have studied Buddhism know that the ten stages of bodhisattvas are:

1. Stage of Joy [Pramudita].
2. Stage of Purity [Vimala], liberation from all forms of defilements.
3. Stage of Luminous Light [Prabhakari], where the radiance of wisdom is generated.
4. Stage of Flaming Wisdom [Arcismati].
5. Stage of Overcoming Utmost Difficulties [Sudurjaya].
6. Stage of Open Way of Wisdom [Abhimukhi].
7. Stage of Far Reaching [Duramgama].

8. Stage of Immovability [Acala].
9. Stage Excellent Wisdom [Sadhumati].
10. Stage of Dharma Cloud [Dharmamegha].

The next stage is perfect enlightenment, [in which the wise being exhibits] thirty two marks of perfection and a vast amount of merits and virtues. Then, wonderful enlightenment, supreme buddhahood, is the following stage. [A buddha with] perfect enlightenment is an eleventh stage buddha , and [a buddha with] wonderful enlightenment is a twelfth stage buddha.

As far as I know, the Thousand-armed Avalokitesvara Bodhisattva has eleven heads. The topmost head is that of Amitabha Buddha, followed by that of Vajrapani, followed by the remaining heads of the Nine-headed Avalokitesvara (symbolizing the eleventh stage). Hence, the Thousand-armed Avalokitesvara is an eleventh stage buddha (The Tathagata Who Clearly Understands the True Law).

Shakyamuni Buddha attained wonderful enlightenment fruition, the four kinds of nirvana, and the perfection of four wisdoms. Hence, he is a twelfth stage buddha. [What about] the Great All-illuminating Sun Tathagata, Mahavairocana Buddha? He attained the perfection of five wisdoms. He is a thirteenth stage buddha (dharmakaya). Last but not least, there is Adi Buddha, who is revered as the Primordial Buddha in Vajrayana Buddhism; he is at the sixteenth stage.

Okay, now Sheng-yen Lu has discovered that there are buddhas above the Primordial Buddha, Adi Buddha. Beyond Adi Buddha, there are buddhas of the seventeenth stage. I deem these buddhas' names to be "Nameless Buddhas." All the buddhas of seventeenth stage are all nameless, formless, action-less, accomplishment-less, and nothing can be used to describe them.

The proper name for all the seventeenth stage buddhas collectively are Nameless Buddhas. You can only really be called the enlightened one after you have discovered the seventeenth stage buddha. That is to say [true nature is] not buddha, not heart, nor object.

If you review the Sutra of Buddhas' Names, there are many buddhas' names mentioned. You will find that many buddhas have the same name. There are quadrillions of buddhas named Lamp-burning Buddha. There are also millions of buddhas named Shakyamuni Buddha. As long as a buddha has a name, he is below the sixteenth stage. The buddhas of the seventeenth stage do not have names. Hence, I call them Nameless Buddhas. I am a genuinely enlightened one, so [I know that it is a fact]; there isn't anything more real than this. Only those who discover the seventeenth stage buddhas are supreme enlightened ones.

> Avalokitesvara Bodhisattva's compassion
> Manjushri Bodhisattva's wisdom
> Vajrapani Bodhisattva's dharma power
> Compassion, wisdom, plus dharma power
> Equals the genuine reality

Those who realize the infinite and boundless nameless buddhas have genuine enlightenment!

Sheng-yen Lu

30. Did I Denigrate Shakyamuni Buddha?

A monk was shocked by my writings on "The Buddhas of the Seventeenth Stage." He told me, "Grand Master Lu, Shakyamuni Buddha is the founder of Buddhism, the World Honored One, and most revered of all. Yet, you ranked him as a twelfth stage buddha, that is lesser than the Buddhas of the Seventeenth Stage, aren't you denigrating Shakyamuni Buddha?"

I responded, "No."

The monk continued, "The Great All-illuminating Sun Tathagata is a thirteenth stage buddha; Shakyamuni Buddha is of the twelfth stage; Adi Buddha is of the sixteenth stage. Hasn't Shakyamuni Buddha been denigrated?"

I answered, "The Great All-illuminating Sun Tathagata (Vairocana Buddha) is a dharmakaya buddha, the source of all buddhas. Shakyamuni Buddha is also one of them, and they are one and the same. In reality, they are all equal. With regard to the sixteenth stage Adi Buddha, that is the view of some people in Vajrayana Buddhism, and not everyone shares this view. So, Adi Buddha is not included in the discussion.

Then, the monk asked, "What about Grand Master Lu's buddhas of seventeenth stage?"

I answered, "The collective name of the buddhas of the seventeenth stage is 'Nameless' Buddhas. Since they are nameless, formless, action-less, accomplishment-less, non-phenomenal, nothing can describe them, so why would they fight over what stage they are ranked as?"

The monk became relieved after hearing my explanation.

He asked, "Does Shakyamuni Buddha know about the buddhas of the seventeenth stage?"

I answered, "Yes."

"How do you know?" the monk responded.

I answered, "Shakyamuni Buddha said, 'Inexpressible, I didn't utter one word, there is no Dharma to explain, no Dharma to teach.' That is none other than nameless buddhas."

The monk said, "Some say there are ten stages within buddhahood. How would you explain that?"

I answered, "Ten stages of buddhahood are equally attained by buddhas. The distinction lies in their buddha-virtues, not in nature of superiority or inferiority, hence these ten stages are equal."

The Ten Stages of Buddhahood are listed as below:

1. Stage of Profound and Unfathomed Wisdom
2. Stage of Inconceivable Majesty of Pure Body
3. Stage of Virtuous Clear Moon banner Jewel-appearance Sea Treasury
4. Stage of Sublime Golden Radiance Merits and Virtue Miraculous Power Wisdom Virtue
5. Stage of Fire Wheel Majestic Treasury Wisdom Virtue
6. Stage of The Radiance of Non-defiled Flame in Vast Space
7. Stage of Supreme Dharmadhatu Luminous Treasury Realm
8. Stage of Supreme Wisdom of Universal Realization Treasury Capable of Purifying All Defilements Wisdom

9. Stage of Infinite Majestic Dedication Illuminated
10. Stage of Ocean of Vairocana Wisdom Treasury

I said, "The ten stages of buddhas doesn't mean there are different levels of buddha fruitions, but they represent differences in virtues. In reality, they are all equal. These ten stages are different from the ten stages of the bodhisattvas. After attaining buddhahood, all the ten stages can be reached."

In the *Sutra of Buddhas' Names* taught by Shakyamuni Buddha, there were many instances of buddhas sharing the same names, such as the thirty-six trillion, one hundred and nineteen thousand five hundred buddhas named Amitabha Buddha. There are many other buddhas sharing the same name. Those who realize the infinite and boundless nameless buddhas have genuine enlightenment!

In essence
Everyone is equal
This means buddha-nature is innate in everyone
All beings with awareness have buddha-nature

There isn't just one Shakyamuni Buddha. As long as you achieve the same enlightenment as Shakyamuni Buddha in your cultivation, you are a Shakyamuni Buddha.

Sheng-yen Lu

31. Transmigration is Reenacting the Past

In this chapter, I want to discuss one of life's realities.
Ananda once suggested to the Buddha, "O' Buddha, let us move away from this place full of slanders and accusations."

Shakyamuni Buddha replied, "It is the same wherever you go. Do you believe that there is a place which is free of slanders and accusations?"

Ananda responded, "Nowhere will the Buddha not be slandered."

Buddha responded, "Yes, slanders and accusations are reenacted everywhere."

Buddhists know of the defamations and vilifications that Shakyamuni Buddha had to endure while residing in the human world. He was defamed by women, kings, ordinary people, students who betrayed him, etc. Despite of the slander and false accusations swirling around him, Shakyamuni Buddha patiently endured in this World of Patient Endurance.

Today, I, Grand Master Lu, am acting in the same manner. Some students advised me to leave Seattle because of the false rumors circulating in the area. I asked them to name a place that is free of slanders and accusations. My students said, "The North Pole." I asked,

"Are there people living in the North Pole?" They answered, "Yes." I told them, "Wherever there are people, there are false accusations." Like Shakyamuni Buddha, I am patiently enduring in this World of Patient Endurance. (The Saha world is none-other-than the World of Patient Endurance).

I said: There isn't just one Shakyamuni Buddha. As long as you achieve the same enlightenment as Shakyamuni Buddha in your cultivation, you are a Shakyamuni Buddha. Your body is that of the Buddha, your speech is that of the Buddha, and your mind is that of the Buddha. It is as if you reincarnated to reenact the role of Shakyamuni Buddha. Just look, the slanders and false accusations are the same; the experiences are the same; and even the enlightenment is the same. I want everyone to expand their vision to see the infinite and boundless universe. Expand your mind beyond the past, present, and future.

I say who isn't a buddha? Who isn't a reincarnated person? Transmigration in cyclic existence is just the same people reenacting the same theatrical play. The essence of the theatrical play is the same. Only the props are different. If you clearly recognize that transmigration in cyclic existence is the same as continuously reenacting the past, you should reflect back for a moment. Reflect back for a moment, and you will see the scenery of the original ground!

> Dissonant emotions are not dissonant emotions
> No dissonant emotions are dissonant emotions
> Dissonant emotions are Bodhi
> Transmigration in cyclic existence is nirvana

32. The Great Mara

During his time on earth, Master Hsuan Hua (Reverend To Lun) liked to say, "Sheng-yen Lu is a great deva mara." Someone also published a book titled *The Devil of the Religious Community*. The devil in the title refers to Sheng-yen Lu. Many senior members of the Buddhist community [in Taiwan] also say "Sheng-yen Lu is a mara." I never concern myself with these criticisms. This is because no one understands the great mara better than I do.

Based on my knowledge, the great deva mara is the Mara King Papiyan. Papiyan was the Mara King who tried to prevent Shakyamuni Buddha from attaining enlightenment. Papiyan was also the one who advised Shakyamuni Buddha to enter into nirvana [immediately after enlightenment]. Papiyan once again requested the Buddha to enter nirvana when the Buddha was old. The Buddha finally obliged and entered nirvana.

Just who is this Papiyan?

Some people said that Papiyan is the great deva mara! Some people said Papiyan is a bodhisattva dwelling in inconceivable liberation. The residence of the great deva mara is the highest heaven of the desire realms, the sixth heavens of desire realm, the Paranirmita-vasavartin

Heaven. This is the pinnacle of the desire realm heavens!

This Paranirmita-vasavartin heaven is very stately. In that heaven, there is a magnificent palace called the Great Auspicious Jeweled Palace That is Often Visited by All Tathagatas.

Enchanted with celestial music from the bells and drums, decorated with silk drapes and victory banners, and elaborately adorned by pearls, precious gems, and half-moon disc mirrors, the supreme palace of desire exhibits peerless beauty.

Papiyan's heaven in the sixth heaven of the desire realm is where all tathagatas often visit for fun. In this Paranirmita-vasavartin heaven, the Great All-illuminating Sun Tathagata taught the *Scripture that Transcends Principles* also known as the *Adhyardhasatika Prajnaparamita Sutra* (or *Prajnaparamita-naya-satapancasatika*). The six desire heavens and the four dhyana heavens of the form realms amount to ten heavens. These ten heavens represent generosity, discipline, patience, diligence, meditation, wisdom, skillful means, aspirational vow, strength, and knowledge, which are the ten paramitas.

The sixth heavens of the desire realm represent wisdom. Is this a joke that the great Mara King Papiyan represents wisdom?

The desire mara is wisdom; wisdom is the desire mara.

This may be puzzling and people can't understand or figure it out! The one who possessed the greatest desire and forsaken the greatest desire was none-other-than Shakyamuni Buddha. If you are an enlightened one, please tell me who is the great deva mara?

> All the knowledge and wisdom of this world
> Are just dust from the journey
> The entire canon of Buddhist scriptures is just dust from the journey
> When you shake off all the dust from the journey
> You will discover there is only skillful means

Then, you have achieved enlightenment
Explaining it in this way, do you understand?

This is a non-dual world, a state of realization
that is without others and self.

Sheng-yen Lu

33. A Non-Dual World

I pondered these questions for a long time: Why did the Great All-illuminating Sun Tathagata teach the Scripture that Transcends the Principle in the Paranirmita-vasavartin Heaven (heaven of the mara king)? Why did the Great All-illuminating Sun Tathagata teach the Tattvasamgraha Tantra in Akanistha Heaven? Why is the Palace of Paranirmita-vasavartin Heaven known as the Great Auspicious Jeweled Palace that is Often Visited by All Tathagatas? Why do all the tathagatas often visit the heavens of the mara king for amusement?

Tathagatas are buddhas; deva maras are maras. Are buddhas and maras one and the same?

Tathagatas are holy; deva maras are ordinary. Is holy and ordinary one and the same?

This is a non-dual world, a state of realization that is without others and self. Why? Why? Why?

There is one statement that everyone should pay attention: "Because the innate nature of all phenomena is purity, Prajnaparamita is purity as well."

A buddha once threw me into a great swamp where I quickly became trapped and sunk deeper and deeper to the point that my head was about to be submerged. A dakini flew by overhead trying to rescue me at the time. She pulled on my outstretched hands but to no avail because I had already sunk too deep. Then, I suddenly found myself in the air and the swamp around me had vanished. I saw a clean running river and wanted to wash off the mud off my body. But, I shockingly discovered there was no need for cleansing because there was no mud on my body. Hence, I realized, "Because the innate nature of all phenomena is purity, Prajnaparamita is purity as well."

I am reminded of a story about Zen Master Xiantian being visited by Monk Luoping.

Master Xiantian asked, "Where did you come from?"

Monk Luoping responded, "Nanxi!"

Master Xiantian asked, "Is there any 'xiaoxi' [meaning "information"] on Nanxi?"

Monk Luo ping responded, "Xiao [meaning "eliminate"] is already eliminated, xi [meaning "rest"] is not rested."

Master Xiantian said, "The worst suffering is not rested."

Monk Luoping asked, "Why don't you explain what is not rested?"

Master Xiantian said, "Saw the face once, forgot the name after a millennium."

I feel that this phrase "Saw the face once, forgot the name after a millennium" is very interesting.

I wonder whether my noble students understand it or not?

If we meet face-to-face, you would know that I am Sheng-yen Lu. But, after a thousand years, would you still know who Sheng-yen Lu is? I know who you are. But, a thousand years from now, would I still know who you are?

That's it. That's it. Have you figure it out?

34. Vajrayana Buddhism's Offerings

In my personal cultivation of Vajrayana sadhanas, I place great importance on offering practices. Offering practices include the outer offering, inner offering and secret offering.

Let's first talk about outer offerings. Every day, we make material offerings of flowers, incense, lights, tea, fruits, soapy water, conch shells, and scented powders. These are called the eight offerings. Visualize these offerings multiplying into infinity during the offering. Then, there are the thirty-seven offerings which are also outer offerings. Also, if we see beautiful sceneries, it can also be used as an offering. Fire homa offering, water offering, and feast offering, all of them are outer offerings.

Next, let's talk about inner offering. Inner offerings are the offering of five meats and five nectars. In general, the five meats and five nectars of Vajrayana are the secret essences of one's body. This aspect of the offering requires superior understanding and transcendence. If you don't have superior understanding and transcendence, it is impossible to practice the inner offering. The five meats are .... The five nectars are ....

Let us talk about secret offerings! Generally, secret offerings are not revealed. Examples of secret offerings include: making an offering of your secrets to your revered vajra guru, making an offering of a consort, and making an offering of bliss. This type of offering embodies realization of the nature of emptiness. The secret essence within is that there is no person making the offering, no vajra master receiving the offering, and no practice of the offering.

Through this kind of offering (secret offering), "the non-duality of bliss and emptiness" is proven. Through the secret offering, one experiences the truth of no self-nature and that everything is pure. The secret offerings can be said to be a concept. The person making the offering is a concept. The person receiving the offering is a concept. The practice of offering is a concept. No cultivator, no cultivation, nothing exists.

The Buddha said, "All that exist are established as expedient means. Its nature is emptiness."

This is the reason that I was able to attain enlightenment. I can see Shakyamuni Buddha, visit the Great Thunder Temple, and reach any buddha field – demonstrating realization of the supreme truth. Enlightenment! Enlightenment! Enlightenment!

Zen Master Puguan used his hand to expose his chest and asked, "What is this about?"

A monk responded, "That still exists."

Zen Master Puguan then concealed his chest with his hands and said, "That was too revealing."

The monk replied, "What is there to conceal?"

Today Grand Master Lu said all this, "Was this revealing or concealing? Have you figured it out?"

No cultivator, no cultivation, nothing exists

35. Beyond Ethics and Moral Values

We know that good and virtuous people are worthy of respect. Why are they good? It is because they uphold moral values. Why are they virtuous? It is because they are ethical.

Morals and ethics are also very highly regarded in religion. Many religions play important roles in promoting and advancing moral values and ethics. Some exemplary people not only uphold moral values and ethics, they completely dedicate their lives to charitable works. The merits they garner from these deeds are as enormous as the sky. Their charitable contributions are legendary, benefiting people all over the world. Some examples are Mother Teresa of the Catholic Church and Buddhism's Master Cheng Yen of the Tzu Chi Foundation.

But, even if they reach the ideal of religion's highest moral values and ethical principles, does that mean they are enlightened? The answer is not necessarily.

What is enlightenment? It is beyond moral values and ethical principles.

Here, I want to emphasize three points:

1. I am definitely not suggesting that people disregard moral values.
2. I am definitely not advising people to ignore ethical principles.
3. I am definitely not telling people to do bad deeds.

Yet, enlightenment is not on the side of good. Of course, it is also not on the side of evil.

The state I have attained is the one that realizes the "Equality of All Phenomena Vajra Samadhi." I am liberated in all phenomena and feel great boundless joy.

Within this equality of all phenomena, I have already united as one with all sentient beings; in addition, all sentient beings live within me as well. There is neither the hindrance of dissonant emotions, nor the hindrance of the false cognitive view of reality. This is the Wisdom of Equality in Nature.

People say that I am a bad person, a non-Buddhist heathen, a cult leader, not enlightened, a fake living buddha. People have also spread lies about me far and wide. Even with all these attacks, I still feel great boundless joy.

Why? Because of the Equality of All Phenomena Vajra Samadhi.

Zen Master Shigong [who was a hunter before taking up Buddhism] likes to use the unconventional metaphor of shooting an arrow from a drawn bow to direct a cultivator to enlightenment. Master Yizhong paid Master Shigong a visit one day.

Master Shigong drew his bow and said, "On [your] guard!"

Master Yizhong bared his chest asking, "This is an arrow that takes life. How do you shoot an arrow that give life?"

Master Shigong responded by flicking the bowstring three times. Then, Yizhong bowed and thanked Master Shigong for his guidance.

Master Shigong replied, "I've only been able to shoot one half-enlightened man in these thirty years of drawing my bow."

I am giving everyone a clue: What is a half-enlightened person? Is Mother Teresa is half- enlightened? Is Master Cheng Yen half-enlightened? Then, what kind of person is fully enlightened? Try to explain it to me.

What I mean is that as long as you become enlightened in this lifetime, the current world is a pure land.

Sheng-yen Lu

36. Enlightenment in This Very Lifetime

A Buddhist nun asked me, "I have been cultivating for forty years. How much longer do I need to cultivate to be reborn in a pure land?"

I answered, "Where are you now?" (The pure land is everywhere)

She then asked, "How many more lifetimes do I need to cultivate before becoming a buddha?"

I answered, "What are you now?" (This body is that of the Buddha)

The nun said, "You did not answer my questions."

I told her, "I have already answered you."

She said, "I don't understand your answers."

I responded, "I understand them even less."

My guidance for everyone is this: What I mean is that as long as you become enlightened in this lifetime, the current world is a pure land. In actuality, you don't need to cultivate for very long. Like the Western Paradise of Ultimate Bliss, you can reach it in an instant of thought. This is to say, what place isn't a pure land?

I often say, "I am happy like an immortal!" This is because I am in the pure land.

We don't need to talk about how many lifetimes we need to

cultivate to become buddhas. If you have attained enlightenment and thorough realization, you are a buddha right now. As soon as Shakyamuni Buddha became enlightened under the Bodhi tree, he became the Buddha. That is becoming a buddha in this very lifetime. After Shakyamuni Buddha attained buddhahood, even though he still endured physical afflictions, he was still the Buddha. Even if Shakyamuni Buddha had been infamous, he was still a buddha after attaining enlightenment.

I said, "I am a buddha, the Lotus Light Unhindered Buddha, Liansheng Buddha."

It doesn't matter what other people have to say on this matter, I am still a buddha. In the present lifetime, I realized the Vajra Samadhi of the Equality of all Phenomena. I am one with all sentient beings. I am one with all buddhas. Myself, sentient beings, and buddhas, all three are completely equal. You don't need too much time. You don't need to wait too many lifetimes. I am a buddha. I wonder if everyone can understand my explanation in this manner?

When Zen Master Yizhong was a still common monk, he said to Zen Master Dadian, "Don't point to the left or right, please just point it out directly."

Zen Master Dadian answered, "A stone man kneels at the mouth of Youzhou River."

Yizhong said, "You are still pointing to the left and right."

Zen Master Dadian answered, "If you are a true phoenix, you don't need to beg toward that side."

Suddenly, Yizhong became enlightened.

Zen Master Yizhong's realization song is as follows:

> This perception of vision and hearing is not true vision and hearing,
> There's no sound or form that can be presented to you.
> If you realize this truth, then all issues are resolved.

What need is there to differentiate truth from its application?

Dear noble students, have you become enlightened yet?

In the end, all differentiations are innately without differentiation. This is the absolute realization.

Sheng-yen Lu

37. Equality, Equality, Equality, Equality, Equality

I wrote the word "equality" five times for the title of this chapter to sing the praise that Mahavairocana Tathagata is marvelous; Aksobhya Tathagata is marvelous; Ratnasambhava Tathagata is marvelous; Amitabha Tathagata is marvelous; and Amoghasiddhi Tathagata is marvelous. They are the embodiment of the five kinds of wisdoms: the Wisdom of Ultimate Reality, the Great Mirror-like Wisdom, the Wisdom of Equality in Nature, the Wisdom of Discerning Awareness, and the All-accomplishing Wisdom.

These five wisdoms represent five kinds of realizations: Purity, vajra, essence, dharma, and karma. The end results are the equality of the inconceivable purity; the equality of the inconceivable vajra; the equality of the inconceivable essence of doctrines; the equality of the inconceivable dharma; and the equality of the inconceivable karma.

All sentient beings possess the innate purity; all sentient beings are absolutely indestructible [vajra]; all sentient beings fully possess the essence of the same value; all sentient beings have equality in their intrinsic natures; and all sentient beings innately are one.

These are my realizations of purity, vajra, essence, dharma, and karma. In the end, all differentiations are innately without differentiation. This is the absolute realization.

I am reminded of the reason that Mahavairocana Tathagata formed the Supreme Wisdom Mudra. The Supreme Wisdom Mudra is formed by the right hand holding the left hand's index finger, with the right thumb on the top of the left index finger, joining the left and right hands together. This is mutual equality, equality, equality, equality, and equality. Having expressed it this way, I think that those students with great capacity should have grasped the meaning. Yet, the students with less capacity may still be confused.

Aye, how should I phrase this?

Everyone should carefully reflect on Zen Master Benkong's verse:

> Heart is the body of innate nature,
> Innate nature is the application of the heart.
> Heart and innate nature are one and the same,
> What difference is there between them?
> Myriad external appearances obscured the origin,
> Just too difficult for one to comprehend.
> The past and present ordinary and noble beings,
> Are no different than illusions and dreams.

I used the nature of the nose to guide a monk:

I asked the monk, "What is your nose for?"

He replied, "To smell."

I inquired, "If you cover your nose, does the fragrance still exist?"

He replied, "I won't be able to smell it."

I asked, "Does the fragrance still exist?"

He answered, "It is still there."

I told him that it doesn't matter whether he has a nose or not, or whether he is able to smell or not, the fragrance is still there. If you have some realizations, please write an essay on the topic of "What is differentiation? What is non-differentiation?"

38. Where is Emptiness?

A monk asked me, "Which ten traits must a fully qualified vajra master possess?"
I answered:

1. Extensive practice of meditation leading to a tranquil mind under all circumstances.
2. Extensive cultivation of wisdom, with wisdom as great as a vast ocean.
3. Extensive cultivation of the heart, with exceptional ethics and moral values.
4. Possess greater accomplishments than his students.
5. Eagerly assist all sentient beings.
6. Extensive knowledge and understanding of Buddhist scriptures and doctrines.
7. Eloquent and well-versed in debating.
8. Set exemplary standards for others to follow.
9. Complete the cultivation of the four dhyana stages of meditation.
10. Experience and realize the nature of emptiness.

A fully qualified vajra master must possess these ten traits.

Our True Buddha School's vajra masters should diligently work on all ten of these traits. If there are vajra masters missing one or more of these ten traits, they are just ordinary masters. Students of ordinary masters will not have great accomplishments. If we are stringent, very few people in today's world actually meet the qualifications of having perfected all ten of these traits to be a vajra master. The tenth trait, that of experiencing and realizing the nature of emptiness, is the trait that is most especially lacking which very, very few have perfected.

I once went shopping with Master Lianji at the First Square Shopping Center in Taichung, Taiwan. We saw two shirts, both with the Chinese character, "kong" [emptiness], printed in the center.

I said, "These two shirts are fantastic. You can wear the word of emptiness to experience the nature of emptiness."

Unexpectedly, the female shop owner coldly stated, "Emptiness is not worn on the body."

Master Lianji responded, "How can you make such a remark?"

I laughed and said, "This store owner is truly extraordinary; emptiness truly cannot be worn on the body."

Then I asked her, "Where is emptiness?" She didn't answer. Both Master Lianji and I asked her several times again, "Where is emptiness?" But, she still refused to answer. I ended up buying both shirts. Later, I discovered this female shop owner was a Buddhist and there was even a small Buddhist shrine in the shop.

Emptiness is most sublime. If you seek to experience and awaken to emptiness, [you may] encounter difficulty with this word, emptiness, like many people would. The emptiness that we are talking about is not a vacuum in the material world; not the literal word, emptiness; not the conceptualization of emptiness in the mind; not the emptiness which is the opposite of substantiality; not meaningless banter on emptiness; not negating emptiness; and not an emptiness that is nurtured.

Now I would like to ask a question to test my noble students. If I were to ask you, "Where is emptiness?" How would my noble students answer this question?

> Desire is empty
> Fame and social standing are empty
> Precious metals and jewelry are empty
> Sexual desire is empty
> Indulging in desire is empty
> Even if you believe that you own these desires and possessions
> In reality
> The result is also emptiness

All the knowledge and wisdom of this world are all just dust from this journey. The entire collection of Buddhist scriptures are all just dust from this journey. When you shake off all the dust from this journey, discovering that they are only expedient means, then you can be considered enlightened.

Sheng-yen Lu

39. Three Wise Monkeys

I once saw wooden statues of the three wise monkeys in a craft store. Each of these three monkeys held a different pose. The first monkey covered its eyes, the second one covered its ears, and the third monkey covered its mouth.

These three monkeys symbolize: see no evil, hear no evil, and speak no evil. I found them very interesting and they reminded me of a passage in the *Heart Sutra*: "no eye, no ear, no nose, no tongue, no body, no mind; no appearance, no sound, no smell, no taste, no touch, no phenomena."

If a wood carver could create a representation of covering the nose, the body, and the mind, then it would be much more interesting. I think the carving a monkey covering his nose is relatively simple, but coming up with a way to show the covering the body and or the covering of the mind would be much more difficult.

Generally, members of the Yogacara [Mind-only] school advocate non-existence of the external world and that everything is derived from the mind. Their cultivations focus on consciousness. Through cultivation of the eye, ear, nose, tongue, body, and mind consciousnesses, they then enter the seventh consciousness, manas consciousness (the root of the mind). Subsequently, they enter into the eighth consciousness, the alaya consciousness (tathagatagarbha consciousness).

Someone claimed to have reached the state of the alaya consciousness and also claimed that the ninth consciousness, amala consciousness, and the tenth consciousness, pristine consciousness, are all just variations in the name of the eighth consciousness.

This person claimed to be enlightened and accused other schools' cultivators as being non-enlightened and having false realization. He is especially biased against the Prasangika-Madhyamaka school.

Different sects of Buddhism include the Madhyamaka School (which is further divided into the Prasangika-Madhyamaka School and the Svatantrika-Madhyamaka School), the Yogacara School, the Sautrantika School, etc.

Frankly, I have also realized the stage of the alaya consciousness, having personally validated each of the eight consciousnesses. I have completely comprehended the five categories of name and form, the three natures in which we perceive the world, the seven perfections, the seven characteristics of a Buddha's nature, and the two categories of anatman.

I personally believe attaining the stage of the alaya consciousness is not a big deal. Attaining the stage of the alaya consciousness isn't enlightenment.

The *Heart Sutra* states, "no eyes, ears, nose, tongue, body, mind."

Cultivating using the mind and reaching the stage of the alaya consciousness can only be described as being close to enlightenment.

This person commented that many Zen cultivators have realized the true nature of the heart, but very few of them have seen their Buddha-nature. I personally have this question, "How can you be so certain that many people have realized the nature of heart but few have seen their Buddha-nature? Are you saying that the Yogacara School is the only path to supreme truth?"

I personally believe:

> Learning Buddhism (is just dust from this journey).
> Buddhist studies (are just dust from this journey).
> The Madhyamaka School (is just dust from this journey).
> The Yogacara School (is just dust from this journey).
> The Sautrantika School (is just dust from this journey).

All the knowledge and wisdom of this world are all just dust from this journey. The entire collection of Buddhist scriptures are all just dust from this journey. When you shake off all the dust from this journey, discovering that they are only expedient means, then you can be considered enlightened. Do you understand my explanation? (The reason behind Shakyamuni Buddha's statement that he had never said one word is right here).

Perfect enlightenment intrinsically exists. The perfect enlightenment I have attained is none-other-than "nothing to gain". It is because I realized that there is "nothing to gain", hence that is real attainment. This is the language of non-arising.

Sheng-yen Lu

40. Speaking the Language of "Non-arising" in Unison

At the time of my awakening, I realized I had attained perfect enlightenment. Hence, I shouted "Oh heavens! Oh heavens!" If we distilled the enlightenment that Shakyamuni Buddha attained while seated under the bodhi tree into a simple phrase, it would be, "So that's how it is! That's how it is!" If we shorten the phrase even more, then it would be "All are buddhas! All are buddhas!"

Shakyamuni Buddha's statements on "non-arising" were: "All things are impermanent"; "All phenomena are without self-nature"; and "Nirvana is perfect quiescence." Finally, his most important statements on "non-arising" were: "I never taught any dharma!" "I never even uttered a word!" "There were no three turnings of the dharma wheel. I never turned the dharma wheel, not even once." These three "non-arising" statements contain the most important absolute truth that Shakyamuni Buddha realized. Hence, the Buddha said, "If someone claims that the Buddha had given any teachings, he is defaming the Buddha."

Here I want make this emphatically clear. If anyone says,

"Shakyamuni Buddha was born in the saha world; went through stages of birth, renouncing the world, cultivating for supreme truth, attaining enlightenment, becoming the Buddha, turning the dharma wheel three times, and entering nirvana," I would respond, "That's nonsense! Rubbish!!" The so-called Shakyamuni Buddha isn't Shakyamuni Buddha, which is precisely Shakyamuni Buddha.

Today, if someone asks me, "Sheng-yen Lu, did you write two hundred books?" I would answer, "I have never written any books."

If the person asks, "Sheng-yen Lu, did you teach Buddha-dharma for nearly forty years?" I would answer, "I have never taught any Dharma."

If he asks, "Sheng-yen Lu, did you deliver millions of sentient beings?" I would answer, "I have never delivered any sentient being, not even one."

If someone asks, "Sheng-yen Lu, did you establish True Buddha School?" I would answer, "What is True Buddha School?"

If someone asks, "Are you not Sheng-yen Lu?" I would answer, "Who is Sheng-yen Lu? Who is Sheng-yen Lu?"

Today, I am telling everyone forthrightly that I only speak the truth. I don't lie or make up stories. I am very clear on what I say. I have "not arisen," buddhas have "not arisen," sentient beings have "not arisen."

[True nature] is not heart, buddha, or objects.

Perfect enlightenment intrinsically exists. The perfect enlightenment I have attained is none other than "nothing to gain". It is because I realized that there is "nothing to gain", hence that is real attainment. This is the language of non-arising. Does everyone understand? (This is the most important chapter.)

41. Repeatedly Reflecting on "Nothing to Gain"

Frankly, my realization came from repeated reflection on the following passage:

No wisdom, no gain, since there is nothing to gain, Bodhisattva.

This is the passage. It is this short passage. Condense it even shorter, and then we have "nothing to gain." Its meaning overwhelmed me with so much sorrow that I fainted. This term, "nothing to gain," encompasses the great earth, the entire universe, history and civilization, infinite time, succession of world powers, heroes and legends, kings and commoners, saints and bandits, patriots and traitors, and greedy and corrupted ministers. All of them have vanished into a great deluge; there was nothing to gain for all of them.

With "nothing to gain," I discovered the heart of renunciation, bodhicitta, and the proper view of the Middle Way. Buddha-dharma is Buddha-dharma because it possesses the three qualities of the heart of renunciation, bodhicitta, and the proper view of Madhyamaka.

The heart of renunciation – I teach sentient beings to leave this transient world.

The heart of bodhicitta – I teach sentient beings to aspire a heart of bodhicitta.

The proper view of Madhyamaka – I teach sentient beings to practice nothing to gain.

I emphasize the heart of renunciation, bodhicitta, and the proper view of the Middle Way because I have fully realized the meaning of nothing to gain.

A great root vajra master doesn't just have wisdom as vast as the ocean, but he also has achieved the realization of nothing to gain. This realization is not a mere intellectual realization. The realization manifests in every one of his words and deeds. He is a truly great bodhisattva because he embodies nothing to gain in practice.

An enlightened person understands that all of the desires of this world, the anger of this world, the defilements of this world, the crimes of this world, the phenomena of this world, the sentient beings of this world, the wisdom of all wisdoms of this world, and all prajnaparamitas are all nothing to gain.

Through nothing to gain, we see through anger, greed, offense, and delusion.

From the perspective of nothing to gain, there are no dualistic opposing sides, and everything is equal. This is the world's genuine truth.

A monk asked Zen Master Shandao, "Have you been to Mount Wutai?"

Zen Master Shandao replied, "Yes I have."

The monk asked, "Did you see Manjushri Bodhisattva?"

Shandao said, "Sure."

The monk asked, "What did Manjushri say to you?"

Shandao said, "Manjushri said that my birth parents are deep in the weeds."

Here I ask everyone, "Who, since the beginning of time, has not been deep in the weeds? Have you realized it yet?"

42. Reflecting Repeatedly on "No Big Deal"

I was told that people are using the most widespread and influential forms of mass media to spread the vilest lies about Sheng-yen Lu. These lies are the most despicable slanders, the most calculated defamations, the most unceasing disparagements, and the most unrelenting character assassinations. Someone asked me, "What is it worth to you?" I answered, "Worthless" (I will not give in to extortion). People have asked me, "Aren't you intimated?" I replied, "I have no fear." "Why not?" I answered, "It is 'not a big deal.'"

Many people have thought that Sheng-yen Lu was finished this time. He would certainly be dragged down. Sheng-yen Lu couldn't get out of this mess. He could never bounce back. Sheng-yen Lu was going to be buried alive. He might as well just commit suicide and be done with it.

However, I ate well, slept well, and was full of energy! I was spreading the Buddha-dharma with more vigor, and my teachings were even more splendid. My life became more eventful, laughing every day. Why was this so? This was because I had realized "non-arising." Since [everything did] not arise, [everything is] no big deal.

Today, I say, "Shakyamuni Buddha actually never existed. He was never born into the human world. He never became a monk. He never attained enlightenment, and he neither taught any dharma, nor entered nirvana. Do you believe it?"

Everyone would answer "I don't believe it."

Today I say, "This person Sheng-yen Lu was never born, never cultivated [the Buddha-dharma], never established True Buddha School, never achieved enlightenment, never gave any teachings, and was never slandered. He was never born, hence he will never die. Do you believe it?"

Everyone would answer, "No."

Yet, what everyone doesn't know is that I believe it (I genuinely know this to be true).

This is because I have realized non-arising. Since everything is non-arising, naturally there would be nothing to gain; naturally everything is no big deal; naturally there's "not abiding anywhere." Today, I will let everyone know that I have already attained infinite comprehension. This infinite comprehension is enlightenment. I have already written it as clear as day. If you still don't get it, I'll hit you with a stick. I'll roar at you with a deafening shout. I will beat you until your butt is swollen. You are really upsetting me.

Great masters and teachers, do you get it yet?

43. Repeatedly Reflecting on "Not Abiding Anywhere"

With the realization of non-arising, one recognizes that the desire, form, and formless realms never came to being. Hence, the dissonant emotions of the desire, form, and formless realms are all severed.

There's no need to mention the three lower realms of transmigration: hell, hungry ghost, and animal. They never arose in reality. The asura realm never arose in reality. Even the twenty-eight heavens never really arose in reality. All the pure lands created by transformations of buddhas and bodhisattvas never arose in reality. Hence, all the dissonant emotions of these places of dwelling are completely severed. This becomes "not abiding anywhere"

The *Vijnaptimatratasiddhi-sastra* says each buddha has four bodies:

1. The self-nature body, which is the dharma body;
2. The reward body for the sake of others, a body that a buddha manifested for the sake of others, revealing his glory to bodhisattvas, enlightening and inspiring them;

3. The reward body, a body manifested by a buddha for his own bliss;
4. A miraculous body of a buddha's transformation.

In addition, the Tiantai school established terminologies of dharma body, reward body, emanation body, and [temporarily] manifested body of the buddha. The emanation body refers to the body which undergoes the eight stages of attaining buddhahood. The temporarily manifested body refers to an incarnation that appears temporarily for a particular purpose. To sum it up, the dharma body is immutable, not coming or going, the buddha of true suchness. Reward bodies are the merit buddhas and the wisdom buddhas. The emanation bodies and temporarily manifested bodies are incarnations of buddhas manifested [for the sake of sentient beings].

After I attained enlightenment, I recognized the emanation and [temporarily] manifested bodies of buddhas are like dreams, illusions, bubbles and shadows; the reward body is like dreams, illusions, bubbles, and shadows; the dharma body is immutable, non-action, non-dualistic, not separating other and self.

I realize abiding everywhere is not abiding anywhere, not abiding anywhere is abiding everywhere.

Dissonant emotions (or klesas) are non-dissonant emotions. Non-dissonant emotions are dissonant emotions.

Dissonant emotions are bodhi; transmigration is nirvana.

I validated: not abiding anywhere, not abiding anywhere, not abiding anywhere; non-arising, non-arising, non-arising.

I have written all these long useless paragraphs. It doesn't matter whether you understand them or not. If you understand them, then you are close to reaching enlightenment. Non-arising, nothing to gain, no big deal, not abiding anywhere are all not enlightenment in reality. They are just close to reaching the supreme truth.

I will give the following guidance.

One day Shishuang was filtering rice.

Zen Master Guishan said, "Do not throw away any offerings from almsgivers."

Shishuang answered, "None should be thrown away."

Guishan found a grain of rice on the floor and said, "You said that you should not throw away anything, so what is this?"

Shishuang was silent.

Guishan continued, "Do not underestimate this small grain. Countless grains of rice will come from just this one grain."

Shishuang asked, "Countless grains will arise from this one grain, but where did this one grain come from?"

Guishan laughed aloud.

Now let me ask everyone, where did this one grain of rice come from? If you answer it right, then you have attained enlightenment. What's your answer?

> Since nothing has arisen
> Naturally, there's nothing to gain
> Naturally, there's no big deal
> Naturally not abiding anywhere
> Abiding everywhere
> Is none other than not abiding anywhere
> Not abiding anywhere, is abiding everywhere

If everyone realizes "nothing happened" and "equality," then everyone is a noble member of the sangha; everyone realizes the nature of the heart and has seen their Buddha-nature; everyone is close to attaining enlightenment.

Sheng-yen Lu

44. Nothing Happened

The *Sutra of the Buddha's Deeds* [*Abhiniskramanasutra*] recorded these events prior to Siddhartha Gautama's enlightenment and becoming Shakyamuni Buddha. The Mara King awoke from a nightmare foreseeing Siddhartha's enlightenment. Mara King's son advised the Mara King to leave Siddhartha in peace. The Mara's daughters attempted to seduce Siddhartha. The Mara King's and his army attacked Siddhartha.

The *Samyukta-ratna-pitaka-sutra* recorded the test of might between the Mara and the Buddha, in which the Mara and his minions failed in their attempt to lift up a jar of holy water before the Buddha.

It also recorded that Mara's daughters tried every ploy in their seductive repertoire on Siddhartha Gautama. They gyrated their voluptuous figures in hypnotic dances, teased the Buddha with the most sensual voice and flirtatious manner. Any ordinary man would find them irresistible and succumb to burning lust and sexual desires. Yet, Siddhartha Gautama's heart was tranquil, innately pure, without defilement or contamination, immovable and immutable. This is seeing through the five desires as "nothing happened."

In the attempted assault of Mara's army on the Buddha, the Mara led an army of four classes of soldiers: elephant riders, cavalry, infantry, and charioteers. Their flags and banners were hoisted high. Their ranks swelled with legions of yaksas archers, pikemen, and swordsmen riding on tens of thousands of elephants, camels, and horse drawn chariots. They howled and charged toward the Buddha like a massive swarm of black clouds.

Shakyamuni Buddha merely touched the ground with a mudra and the Mara's entire army was immediately vanquished. This mudra is called the Earth-Touching Mudra [Bhumyakramana] or Subjugation of Mara Mudra.

In the sutras, Aksobhya Tathagata formed the Earth-Touching Mudra. This mudra is the Supreme Mudra of the Equality of All Dharma. This mudra also implies a profound tranquil state of the heart; original purity; being without defilement; immovable, and immutable. Any attack simply becomes "nothing happened."

Shakyamuni Buddha's victory over the Mara King Papiyan can be summed up as "nothing happened" and "equality." Everyone should reflect upon this: What is "nothing happened?" What is "equality?" They contain profound meanings. If everyone realizes "nothing happened" and "equality," then everyone is a noble member of the sangha; everyone realizes the nature of the heart and has seen their Buddha-nature; everyone is close to attaining enlightenment.

One time, I was lying down facing the wall. King Mara Papiyan appeared and massaged my arched back. I was unmoved. The Mara said, "Something big just happened. I destroyed your enterprise of delivering sentient beings." I answered, "Nothing happened, nothing really happened." The Mara said, "Why don't you take a look?" I answered, "That's the way it is, it is that way whether I take a look or not. If it is destroyed, it is the same. If it is not destroyed, it is still the same." Out of options, the Mara left.

I have realized that nothing ever happened. I ask my noble students, "What did I realize by realizing nothing ever happened?"

Where will I be after I die
Intrinsically deathless
That is the scenery of the original ground
Never came, also never left
There was no real birth.
Also, there is no real death
Nothing intrinsically ever happens.

The *Lalitavistara Sutra* says, "After the Buddha attained enlightenment, he said, 'I realize the truth of tranquil nirvana. Others cannot possibly comprehend if I were to explain it to them. Hence, I stay silent.'"

Sheng-yen Lu

45. What Are the Signs of Enlightenment?

The *Lalitavistara Sutra* states, "The bodhisattva sat under a tree, having already defeated Mara's fury, accomplished supreme enlightenment, hoisted the great dharma banner, and transcended the three realms. He sat silently under the tree demonstrating the four dhyana meditations as the path of enlightenment for future generations. Purification of thoughts is the first dhyana meditation. Quiet one-pointed focus is the second dhyana meditation. Purifying oneself and seeing genuine reality is the third dhyana meditation. The mind not clinging to good or evil, nor suffering or bliss, living in the moment, tranquil and unchanging is the fourth dhyana meditation. These are the non-action paths for delivering sentient beings. He had already forsaken the source of evil; had no greed, anger, or ignorance; had already ended cycles of birth and death; had already severed the seeds of rebirth, and no more seedlings remained; all goals were accomplished, and wisdom was attained. When the bright star appeared, he achieved total realization, the supreme truth, and the most perfect enlightenment. He attained the ten powers, the four fearlessnesses, and the eighteen qualities of buddhas. The enlightenment and realizations of the Buddha are the most sublime and subtle. They are extremely difficult to realize, comprehend, and attain."

In this section of the *Lalitavistara Sutra*, it explains the spiritual attainments of the Buddha:

1. The four dhyanas
2. The ten powers of buddhas [dasabala]
3. The four fearlessnesses
4. The eighteen qualities of buddhas [Avenikadharma]
5. Supreme perfect enlightenment.

In my personal Vajrayana cultivations, I experienced visualizing myself as the personal deity buddha (I am the personal deity, the personal deity is me), one and the same without any duality. Enter -- he enters my body. Dwell -- he dwells in my body. Merge -- he merges into my body.

From the outside, the buddha pride becomes solidified, and the personal deity's features becomes very clear. In the perfection stage: enter -- the qi enters the central channel; dwell -- the qi dwells in the central channel; merge -- the qi circulates throughout and fills the entire body (genuine buddha).

Accomplishments of Vajrayana cultivation:

1. The four dhyanas (samatha)
2. The ten powers of the buddhas [dasabala]
3. The four fearlessness
4. The eighteen qualities of buddhas
5. Supreme perfect enlightenment

The *Lalitavistara Sutra* says, "After the Buddha attained enlightenment, he said, 'I realize the truth of tranquil nirvana. Others cannot possibly comprehend if I were to explain it to them. Hence, I stay silent."

The *Lalitavistara Sutra* also says, "The Buddha told the Great Brahma, 'I have realized the most subtle, profound, and sublime Dharma. Rarely seen or realized, it is supremely tranquil. It is not something that can be deciphered by the discriminating mind. Only buddhas can comprehend this supreme reality. Hence, I am silent.'"

Of course, I understand why the Buddha chose silence in the *Lalitavistara Sutra*.

This is because I know that the four dhyana and eight concentrations, the ten powers, the six miraculous powers, fearlessness, and the eighteen qualities of buddhas are like echoes in mountain gorges, like the moon's reflection in the water, like a flower's image in a mirror, seemingly real but not in actuality, etc.

These are precisely signs of accomplishment. Hence, I observe this world to be: echoes in mountain gorges, reflections of the moon in water, the image of a flower reflecting in a mirror, seemingly real but not really, in the state of deep sleep, in the state of unconsciousness, and to be illusory.

With my enlightenment I have realized: "The most subtle, profound and sublime Dharma is rarely seen or realized. It is supreme tranquility. It is not something that can be deciphered by the discriminating mind. Only buddhas can comprehend this supreme reality. Hence, I am silent."

Dissonant emotions are just dust from our journey. Anything and everything is all supreme purity. That is the original appearance.

Sheng-yen Lu

46. Does this World Exist?

I often wonder if this world (saha world) really exists. Many people found this thought to be puzzling and responded by saying Sheng-yen Lu has gone off to some wild flight of fancy, went mad, is talking crazy, and is hopelessly untreatable.

Let me explain my reasoning with some small examples. A tea cup exists and can hold water. This confirms the existence of the tea cup. But, if the tea cup is broken, it would just be pieces of ceramic, and then this tea cup would no longer exist. A tree exists. But, when a bulldozer knocks it down, not only is the tree gone but so is its former shadow. A house exists. But, after the house is torn down, it becomes a vacant lot and you can't see its former glory.

Let me use some large scale examples to explain it further. Rivers have changed their course. Mountain ranges have moved. Seas have dried to become land, and lands have been flooded to become seas. The Earth's crust has undergone at least seven great cycles. The course of history constantly changes, and many ancient civilizations have vanished into history.

Let's use another example which many have contemplated but no one wants to happen. If a great meteor smashes the Earth into pieces (a meteor colliding with the earth) one day, would history and civilizations still exist? Would nation states exist? Would mankind exist? Would saints exist? Would religions exist? Would people's desires for wealth, sexual pleasure, fame, food, and sleep exist? Would greed, anger, ignorance, doubts, pride, vengeance, love, and feelings still exist? And so on and so forth.

By thinking this way, I reached a supreme state of realization, formless and without any expectation.

Does Shakyamuni Buddha exist?

Does Sheng-yen Lu exist?

Hence, Vajra-dharma Bodhisattva realized the purification of all desires and anger. Vajra-tiksna Bodhisattva realized the purification of all defilements and all offenses. Vajra-hetu Bodhisattva realized the purification of all Dharma and all sentient beings. Vajra-bhasa Bodhisattva realized the purification of the wisdom of all wisdoms, the purity of prajnaparamita.

The human world is a transient world. Dissonant emotions are just dust from our journey. Anything and everything is all supreme purity. That is the original appearance.

When he was about to enter nirvana, Zen Master Daowu said to Zen Master Shishuang, "Something has been on my mind for a long time and is becoming a problem. Who can remove it for me?"

Shishuang replied, "Neither the mind nor this thing is what they seem. Attempting to eliminate them will only aggravate the problem."

Daowu said, "Good! Good!"

Today, I tell everyone, [absolute reality is] "not buddha, not heart, and not object." I wonder if everyone came to some realizations? What did you realize? Explain it to me.

47. Ratnasambhava Buddha's Realization

Zen Master Shishuang saw a monk one day and asked, "Who's your teacher?"

The monk answered, "I am studying with Zen Master Dongshan."

Zen Master Shishuang asked, "What does Dongshan usually teach?"

The monk replied, "Zen Master Dongshan often says that people who seek enlightenment walk from east to west, then walk from west to east. I teach them to go from where there is grass to where there is no grass."

Zen Master Shishuang asked, "Has anybody responded to what Zen Master Dongshan said?"

The monk answered, "No."

Zen Master Shishuang said, "There is grass as soon as you open the door."

The monk returned to Zen Master Dongshan and relayed Shishuang's answer to Dongshan. Startled by the answer, Zen Master Dongshan said, "This Zen Master Shishuang is a great virtuous guide that is rarely found among millions of people."

Ratnasambhava Buddha's realization just happens to be that there is grass as soon as you open the door.

I will give another example.

[Chancellor of the Song Dynasty] Wang Anshi wrote a poem called "Dream" which I like very much.

> Knowing the world is like a dream, I seek nothing.
> Seeking nothing, my heart is empty tranquility.
> Going with the flow of this dream [with equanimity].
> Accomplish dream merits infinitely.

Someone asked me, "Why try to accomplish anything if it is just a dream?"

I answered, "I am just dreaming."

"What are you dreaming of?"

"I dream of being a great accomplished master, of being a person who performs great deeds of merits, and of liberating numerous sentient beings."

(This is Ratnasambhava Buddha's realization).

Someone asked me, "Do the two hundred books you've written have any effect?"

I answered, "None."

"What's the point of writing if it accomplishes nothing?"

I answered, "Write."

He asked again, "Why write if you know it accomplishes nothing?"

I answered, "I write for the sake of writing."

(This is Ratnasambhava Buddha's enlightenment).

Dear readers, in this book I have discussed the subject of emptiness and substantiality, inner and outer, purity and defilement, birth and cessation, transmigration in cyclic existence and nirvana, the noble and the ordinary, good and bad, virtue and evil, etc. Yet, my realization is not within the scope of any of them. My realization is perfect enlightenment.

I manifest sublime effects within the dharma nature. Everything I say contains enlightenment because of this spiritual attainment. I am a genuinely enlightened person and truly liberated. But, Han Shanzi already said it best in his poem, "Nothing is comparable to it. How can I express it?"

As long as you really understand what the word, "Buddha" means, then you wouldn't form any attachment or obscuration with respect to this word "Buddha."

Sheng-yen Lu

48. About the Word "Buddha" in "Liansheng Buddha"

In front of fifty thousand followers at the Putra Stadium of Bukit Jalil, Malaysia, I announced, "I am Liansheng Buddha."

I heard that some people disagreed with my statement.

Some commented, "Claiming enlightenment and realization without achieving neither."

Some turned up their noses.

This word "Buddha" in my statement stirred up a lot of controversies.

At this point, I will give a simple explanation. Despite the difference in appearance between Shakyamuni Buddha and me, our essence is one and the same. What is the relationship between the Buddha and me? In actuality, all enlightened ones know that we are all one and the same. The supreme truth that Shakyamuni Buddha realized is the same as what I have realized. I have examined my awakening in detail and cannot find any difference between mine and that of Shakyamuni Buddha.

On the level of Vajra, Buddha and I are equal. On doctrines, Buddha and I are equal. On Dharma, Buddha and I are equal. On karma, Buddha and I are equal. I am the Buddha, and the Buddha is me.

I also say that it is not just I who is a buddha. Even the most pitiful beggar who doesn't resemble a buddha in appearance whatsoever—everyone is equal. This is to say that everyone is endowed with the same Buddha-nature. This Buddha-nature is possessed by all beings with awareness. I am not the one who originated this declaration. Shakyamuni Buddha declared this when he attained enlightenment.

The fools of this world think that this title, "Buddha," represents authoritativeness. Yet, they would never understand you have to cut off absolute authoritativeness to find the original appearance. As long as you really understand what the word, "Buddha" means, then you wouldn't form any attachment or obscuration with respect to this word "Buddha." You can experience the ultimate truth without any limitation and discover that you are the same as the ultimate reality. Then, you have reached absolute liberation.

I have already realized that I am everlasting. My essence is the Buddha. My teaching is the same as that of the Buddha. My motions are the same as the Buddha. My freedom is the same as that of the Buddha. Realization is infinitely precious. The true reality is infinitely precious.

I don't know if everyone can understand this explanation. Basically, this is the complete unity of all phenomena. The Buddha is contained in my body. The Buddha's body contains me. I, Buddha, and sentient beings [are one and the same] (one undifferentiated unity).

I will give this further guidance.

Someone asked me, "Why do you call yourself a buddha?"

I asked, "If I am not a buddha, then what am I?"

He couldn't answer my question.

Someone asked me, "Why do you tell others that you are a buddha?"

I said to him, "Nothing in the vast emptiness of space or the great expanse of earth is comparable. Hence, using this term, "buddha," is most suitable." (In actuality, even buddha is also emptiness.)

He asked me, "Did you really achieve awakening?"

I answered, "I am not deluded. What did I awaken from?"

"Ha, ha, ha!" I laughed loudly three times.

A wiser student may shout, "Enlightenment is unity of all phenomena."

I would answer, "Unity my butt."

With everyone quiet and silent, I would nod my head and say, "This is the time, this is the time."

I wonder if you understand this chapter on non-arising.

Sheng-yen Lu

49. Speaking on Non-arising Again

Maybe you will let out a big sigh of relief as you come to this last chapter, saying to yourself, "I am finally going to find enlightenment."

If so, I would ask reader A, "Tell me, what do you think enlightenment is?"

Reader A may respond, "Enlightenment is the eighth consciousness, the tathagatagarbha consciousness, realizing this eighth consciousness."

To this I would say, "Way off base. There still remains a consciousness."

Reader B may answer, "Enlightenment is equality of all equality, equality of everything."

To this I would say, "Wrong realization."

Reader C may answer, "Enlightenment is nothing to gain, no big deal, not abiding anywhere."

And I would say, "You are only close."

Reader D may answer, "Awakening is the Five Buddhas and their corresponding Five Wisdoms."

I would respond, "That is not enlightenment at all. Any Buddhist would know about the Five Buddhas and their Five Wisdoms. Just as any Buddhist would also know about the eighth, ninth, and tenth consciousness."

Once again I will ask, "What do you think enlightenment is?"

Reader E may answer, "Madhyamaka [Middle Way] says enlightenment is sublime substantiality within emptiness. Yogacara [Mind-Only] says enlightenment is non-existence of the external world and everything is derived from the mind."

I would say, "You missed."

Reader F may answer, "Enlightenment is not attached to anything, no obscuration, and not even a trace of attachment."

I would say, "No, a trace still remains."

Reader G may answer, "Enlightenment is only one word, 'emptiness.' "

I would say, "That is also not it. That is clinging to an extreme."

Reader H may say, "Enlightenment is only one word, 'buddha.' "

I would reply, "Garbage."

Reader I may say, "Enlightenment is only one word, 'heart.'"

I would respond, "Where is this heart? Tell me, where is this heart?"

Reader J may say, "Enlightenment is formless, without expectation, everything is pristine, and pristine purity of self-nature."

I would say, "Just a bit off."

Reader K may say, "Enlightenment is nowhere to be found, ineffable, never said a word."

I would say, "Almost there!"

Reader L may say, "Enlightenment is just non-arising."

I would say, "Off just ever so slightly."

Reader M may say, "Enlightenment is not buddha, not heart, and not object."

I would say, "This answer is barely acceptable."

Reader N may say, "Enlightenment is like a dream, illusion, bubble, and shadow."

I would say, "Flashes of lightning and fire sparks are not enlightenment."

Reader O may say, "Enlightenment is a flower's reflection in the mirror or a moon's image in water."

I would say, "You also didn't hit it on the mark. You are only treating it as an illusion."

Reader P may say, "Would Grand Master Lu please answer the question? What is enlightenment?"

I would say, "Enlightenment is, it is, it is… Does everyone understand? Reflect upon it. What is this 'it'?"

Then, I would demonstrate the pose, "golden rooster standing on one leg."

A wise student may shout, "Enlightenment is the word 'I.'"

I would reply, "Take a hike!"

A wiser student may shout, "Enlightenment is unity of all phenomena."

I would answer, "Unity my butt."

With everyone quiet and silent, I would nod my head and say, "This is the time, this is the time."

I wonder if you understand this chapter on non-arising.

Glossary

-A-

Absolute Truth
Reality as it is (see *Two Truths Doctrine*).

All Illuminating Sun Tathagata
Commonly translated as the Great Sun Tathagata, Mahavairocana means the great radiant one who illuminates all directions, symbolizing his wisdom piercing all ignorance. Vairocana Buddha is the chief of the Five Wisdom Buddhas and the Lord of the Tathagata Family. He is the embodiment of the wisdom of ultimate reality. He is associated with center direction and the element of space. The symbol of his family is the eight-spoke wheel, the symbol of the noble eightfold path.

Alaya Consciousness (Sanskrit, literally "Abode, Dwelling")
The eighth consciousnesses defined by Yogacara School. This eighth consciousness stores all the actions and experiences from one's lives as karmas. It is unaffected by the death of one's physical body. Hence, karmas follow one from lives to lives exerting influence on the working of seven consciousnesses.

Amala Consciousness (Sanskrit, literally "Pure" or "Undefiled")
The ninth-consciousness which was added later to the Yogacara philosophy to explain Buddha-nature.

Amitabha Buddha (Sanskrit, literally "Boundless light")
The Buddha of Boundless Light and Longevity, he is one of the Five Wisdom Buddhas and the Lord of the Lotus Family. He embodies

the Wisdom of Discerning Awareness which is the antidote to desire and lust. His color is red, element is fire, and direction is west. He is depicted with his hands forming the meditation mudra. Amitabha Buddha's pure land (paradise) is called Sukhavati located in the Western direction. He is the Primary Buddha of the Pure Land Sect and often depicted to be accompanied by his two attendants, Avalokitesvara and Mahasthamaprapta Bodhisattva.

Ananda
A devout attendant and a cousin of Shakyamuni Buddha. During the First Buddhist Council convened to preserve the Buddha's teachings, it was Ananda who recalled and recited the majority of Shakyamuni Buddha's discourses because of his exceptional memory. These discourses became the sutras.

Amoghasiddhi Buddha (Sanskrit, literally "One Who Accomplishes His Goal" or "One whose accomplishment is not in vain".)
One of the Five Wisdom Buddhas and the Lord of the Karma (Action) Family. He embodies the All-Accomplishing Wisdom, the antidote to fear. His element is air, color is green, and direction is north.

Akshobhya Buddha (Sanskrit, literally "Immovable")
One of the Five Wisdom Buddhas and the Lord of the Vajra Family. He embodies the Great Mirror-Like Wisdom which recognizes the inherent emptiness of sense impressions and ideas of individual forms. His wisdom is the antidote to anger and hatred. His element is water, direction is the east, and his color is blue.

Attainment
See *Siddhi*.

Avalokitesvara Bodhisattva (Sanskrit, literally "Lord Who Observe s Sounds of the World")

The embodiment of compassion, Avalokitesvara Bodhisattva compassionately observes the sounds of the world and renders assistance to any devotee who calls out his name. The stories of prayers answered and the myriad miracles performed by Avalokitesvara made him the most widely worshipped bodhisattva. Known as Chenrezig in Tibet, the Tibetan people claim to be his descendents and consider him as their patron bodhisattva. They believe that Chenrezig has appeared many times in Tibet to protect the Buddhist faith. King Songtsan Gampo (the Tibetan king who introduced Buddhism into Tibet) and Dalai Lama are believed by Tibetans to be incarnations of Chenrezig. As result of this special relationship, Avalokitesvara's mantra, Om Mani Padme Hum, is the most widely chanted mantra by the Tibetan people.

Avalokitesvara Bodhisattva is worshipped in China as the female bodhisattva, Guanyin. This change of Avalokitesvara from a male bodhisattva to being depicted as a female one apparently occurred gradually during the Song Dynasty. Some have postulated that Chinese worship Avalokitesvara as a female deity because Chinese culture views compassion as a feminine quality. Guanyin's popularity in China is summed up by the Chinese saying that "The Amitabha Buddha's name is chanted in every house. Guanyin Bodhisattva is worshipped in every home." As Buddhism spread from China into the neighboring Asian countries such as Korea and Japan, Avalokitesvara was introduced to them as Guanyin, a female bodhisattva.

The Buddhist scriptures speak of Avalokitesvara appearing in many forms including the two armed, four armed, or the thousand armed and thousand eyed Avalokitesvara. The scriptures also state that Avalokitesvara will appear in the most suitable form for the circumstances when rendering assistance.

-B-

Bliss Body
See *Three Bodies of a Buddha*.

Bodhi
See *Enlightenment*.

Bodhisattva (Sanskrit, literally "Awakened Being")
An enlightened being (or one who has not achieve full enlightenment) who choose to remain in cyclic existence to assist others to achieve enlightenment.

Brahma (The Creator)
One of the three primary deities of Hinduism. The other two deities are Vishnu (the preserver) and Shiva (the destroyer). He is usually depicted with four heads, four faces, and four arms. Buddhist scriptures recorded that Brahma appeared to Shakyamuni Buddha after the Buddha's enlightenment. Brahma asked the Buddha not to enter nirvana immediately and stay in the human world to spread Buddha-dharma. Hence, Brahma was the first who request the Buddha to "turn the dharma wheel."

Buddha (Sanskrit, literally "Awakened One")
The term is typically used to refer to the historical Buddha, Shakyamuni Buddha. In Mahayana Buddhism, the term, buddha, is not restricted to just Shakyamuni Buddha. It refers to anyone who is enlightened.

Buddha Pride
During the generation stage cultivation, a Vajrayana practitioner is

to develop the conviction that he or she is the personal deity. This is done by visualizing that one's body is that of the personal deity, one's speech is words of the personal deity, and one's thoughts are the perfect wisdom of the personal deity. As a result, the practitioner recognize s the personal deity as none-other-than one's own mind without any fixation or attachment.

-C-

Channels
In energy physiology of Vajrayana, channels are the energy pathways which qi and drops travel in the body. There are three main pathways with central channel being the focus of cultivation. The central channel runs parallel and in front of the spinal cord.

Clear Light
The inner radiance observed by meditation practitioners when they perceive the mind of clear light, which is the most subtle level of awareness. This fundamental level of awareness is a continuum that has no beginning or end. This continuum has no breakage even during death or buddhahood. Experienced cultivators can access the mind of clear light through advanced yoga such as the Yoga of Clear Light. This state of mind allows one to recognize emptiness directly. Ordinary beings experience the mind of clear light momentarily (but the experience is so fleeing that they cannot perceive it) at the time of death, just before falling asleep, etc.

Conventional Truth
The aspect of absolute reality perceived by ordinary perception. Conventional truths are true within certain perspective and scope, but not true in the absolute sense. See *Two Truths Doctrine*.

Consciousness

Also translated as mind and discernment, consciousness is the translation of Sanskrit vijnana. Consciousness in this usage does not refer to the mind. Instead it refers to the sensory based perception and the mind. In early schools of Buddhism, they speak of only six consciousnesses: eye (sight) consciousness, ear (hearing) consciousness, nose (smell) consciousness, tongue (taste) consciousness, body (tactile) consciousness, and mind consciousness. These six consciousnesses together shape our understanding of reality. In the Yogacara School, the six consciousnesses were expanded to eight consciousnesses, and later, nine and ten consciousnesses.

Consciousness Only

See *Yogacara.*

Consciousness Transference

See *Six Yogas of Naropa.*

Cyclic Existence (Sanskrit, literally "Samsara")

The unending successive cycles of rebirths within the Six Realms of Rebirths until one attains liberation and enter nirvana. Sentient beings roam in the six realms of rebirths (heavens of gods, realm of asuras, realm of humans, realm of animals, realm of hungry ghosts, and realm of hell) unaware of their imprisonment life after life. They are constantly propelled by the three poisons of greed, anger, and ignorance to chase after what they believe will bring them happiness but ultimately only find dissatisfaction and disappointment. All the while, their karmic deeds caused by endless grasping, habitual tendencies, and beginningless delusion continuously sow seeds for their rebirth in the six realms, bringing more suffering.

-D-

Dharma
Dharma usually means the body of teachings expounded by the Buddha. The word is also used in Buddhist phenomenology as the term for phenomenon, a basic unit of existence and/or experience.

Dharmakaya
Dharmakaya is Sanskrit for dharma body. See *Three Bodies of Buddha*.

Dharma Body
See *Three Bodies of a Buddha*.

Dharma Wheel
An eight-spoke wheel is a symbol that represents the teachings of Buddhism. "Turning the dharma wheel" is a metaphor for spreading Buddhist teachings.

Dissonant Emotions
The term, dissonant emotions, is the translation for the Sanskrit word "klesa." It means mental distress which obscures the mind causing suffering mentally and physically. This includes mental anguish, stress, paranoia, etc.

Dream Yoga
See *Six Yogas of Naropa*.

Drops
The transcription of Sanskrit bindu referring to vital essences of the body.

-E-

Emanation Body
See *Three Bodies of a Buddha.*

Enlightenment
Enlightenment is the translation of the Sanskrit word, Bodhi, which literally means awakened. Enlightenment is awakened to absolute reality as it is.

-F-

Five Aggregates
See *Five Skandhas.*

Five Elements
The five elements are earth, wind, fire, water, and space.

Five Poisons
The five poisons are ignorance, anger, pride and greed, desire, and jealousy.

Five Precepts
The most basic precepts of Buddhism: (1) do not kill; (2) do not steal; (3) do not commit sexual misconduct; (4) do not lie; (5) and do not take intoxicants.

Five Skandhas
Skandha is Sanskrit for heaps or aggregates. The five skandhas are form, feeling, perception, mental formation, and consciousness. These are psychophysical components of a human being which when interacting together creates the illusion of self and inherent existence of self.

Five Wisdoms
See *Five Wisdom Buddhas*.

Five Wisdom Buddhas
Also known as Five Dhyani Buddhas, the Five Wisdom Buddhas are celestial buddhas visualized in Vajrayana meditations. The five Buddhas are Aksobhya, Amitabha, Amoghasiddhi, Ratnasambhava and Vairocana. Each embodies a different aspect of enlightened consciousness to aid in spiritual transformation: (1) Vairocana Buddha - Wisdom of Ultimate Reality; (2) Akshobhya Buddha - Wisdom of Great Mirror-like; (3) Ratnasambhava Buddha - Wisdom of Equality in Nature; (4) Amitabha Buddha - Wisdom of Discerning Awareness; (5) Amoghasiddhi Buddha - Wisdom of All-accomplishing.

Four Noble Truths
The first and fundamental teaching of Shakyamuni Buddha. These truths are: the truth of suffering, the truth of the accumulation and origin of suffering, the truth of the cessation of suffering, and the truth of the path to the cessation of suffering.

The truth of suffering is that suffering is pervasive in our lives. The eight forms of sufferings are: suffering of birth, suffering of old age, suffering of sickness, suffering of death, suffering of being with that which one despises, suffering of being apart from that which one adores, suffering of not having one's desire fulfill, and suffering of five skandhas flourishing.

The truth of accumulation and origin of suffering is that sufferings are the results of our own doings. Sufferings are brought about by the poisons of greed, anger, and ignorance. Actions propel by them results in the formation of the three realms and six places of rebirths trapping sentient beings in perpetual cycle of life and death.

The truth of cessation is that suffering can be ended by cessation of these cravings.

The truth of the way to end suffering is to practice the noble eight-folded path.

Aspiration for liberation from this cyclic existence comes from the insight to the first and second noble truth. Insight to the third and fourth noble truth enables genuine liberation from karmic bondages.

Four Forms of Births
This is Buddhist terminologies for birth from eggs, dampness, transformation, and womb.

-G-

Generation Stage (Development Stage)
The initial phase of the Vajrayana cultivation after the completion of the preliminary practices. The primary feature of the generation stage is the meditation of the practitioner to identify oneself with the pristine awareness of the meditational deity. This is achieved through a series of visualizations, mantra recitations, and forming of mudras.

Golden Rooster Standing on One Leg
If someone were to ask what Buddha-nature is, Grandmaster Lu said that he would join his palms together in salute and stand on one leg which he called "Golden rooster standing on one leg." This "Golden Rooster pose" is always there and not distinguishing self and other. The standing on one leg reveals a supreme truth. The palms-joined salute also reveals supreme truth.

Golden Mother of the Jade Pond

Ruler of all female immortals, she is the most important female deity of the Daoist Pantheon. Known by many names, such as Queen Mother of the West, she came into being from the gathering of primordial yin (feminine) energy. Her palace is located on top a peak in the Kunlun Mountain Range. She represents the metal element in the Daoist's Five Elements (metal, wood, water, fire, and earth) and there is a Jade Pond near her palace, hence she is also known as the Golden Mother of Jade Pond.

Great Bliss

Great bliss is the blissful state experienced in high level yoga of perfection stage. Great bliss is inexhaustible and arises from the movements of qi (vital energy) in the central channel.

Great Perfection

The supreme tantra of the Nyingma School. Cutting Through Resistance (khregs-chod) and All-Surpassing Wisdom (thodgal) are two of principal practices of Great Perfection. Adepts of Great Perfection have been known for demonstrating rainbow body accomplishment upon their passing, in which their flesh bodies gradually dissolves into five-colored rainbow light leaving hair and nails as the only physical remains.

-H-

Heart

Mind is often referred to as the heart in Chinese Buddhist terminology.

"Heart is the Buddha"

See *Mazu Daoyi*.

Hinayana (Sanskrit, literally "Lesser Vehicle")
A term used by the later Mahayana Buddhists to describe the earliest schools of Buddhism. Since practitioners of the earliest schools of Buddhism focused on seeking liberation for oneself, the Mahayana Schools deemed it to be the lesser vehicle because it did not work for the liberation of all beings.

The only surviving sect of these earliest schools refers to itself as Theravada (School of the Elders) and rejects the name of "lesser vehicle." Theravada also does not recognize the sutras of Mahayana as these sutras were based on teachings of bodhisattvas and buddhas other than the historical buddha, Shakyamuni Buddha. The Theravada tradition continues mostly in Southeast Asia teaching the way to attain liberation is through one's own meditation and living a monastic lifestyle.

Huineng (638 AD – 713 AD)
The Sixth Zen Patriarch of China and a pivotal figure in the spread of Zen Buddhism. Huineng taught in plain language without the use of complex terminologies making his teachings readily accessible. He taught his students to experience reality directly and to forgo dogmas. His teachings were compiled into the *Platform Sutra* which is the only Chinese Buddhist treatise elevated to the status of a Sutra. After Huineng's passing, Zen Buddhism blossomed into five major sects in China becoming a major influence on Chinese and subsequently world culture.

-I-

Illusory Body
See *Six Yogas of Naropa*.

-J-

-K-

Kalachakra Sadhana
This sadhana is a generation stage practice that involves recitation of Kalachakra mantra, visualizing Kalachakra, and forming the Kalachakra mudra.

-L-

-M-

Madhyamaka (Sanskrit, literally "Middle Path")
Nagarjuna founded the Middle Way School based on the teachings of emptiness that all things are empty of inherent existence.

Mahayana Buddhism (Sanskrit, literally "Greater Vehicle")
This style of Buddhism emphasizes the paths and practices of bodhisattvas to altruistically assist sentient beings to attain enlightenment. It consists of sutra and tantra systems for achieving enlightenment. While the sutra system teaches how to go from fundamental ignorance to enlightenment over countless lifetimes, the tantra system teaches one can attain buddhahood in a single lifetime. Pure Land, Zen, Yogacara, Madhyamaka, and Vajrayana are some of the schools of the Mahayana tradition.

Mahakasyapa
One of the primary disciples of Shakyamuni Buddha, he was renowned for his ascetic self-discipline and moral strictness. He was attributed to be the disciple who received transmission of Zen teachings from the Buddha.

Manjushri Bodhisattva

The bodhisattva of wisdom and knowledge. His practices may be used to help gain wisdom, knowledge and eloquence. He is usually depicted as holding the *Prajnaparamita Sutra* and the Sword of Wisdom.

Mantra

A sacred series of syllables. According to Dudjom Rinpoche, the foremost Twentieth Century authority on Nyingma Vajrayana teachings, mantra is the combination of two Sanskrit words, mana and traya. Mana means the mind and traya means protection. Hence, mantra means "protection from the perceptions of the ordinary mind" that obscure absolute reality.

A mantra also represents the pure speech of enlightened beings, buddhas and bodhisattvas. It is one of the three secrets of tathagata (pure body, speech, and mind). In Vajrayana Buddhism, the chanting of the mantra (pure speech) is accompanied by visualization (pure mind) and mudra (pure body) as prescribed in sadhana to transform ordinary body, speech, and mind of a person to the pure body, speech, and mind of a buddha.

Mara (Sanskrit, literally "Death")

It means demons or demonic influences which are essentially the same as the "devil." They manifest in the form of greed, anger, ignorance, jealousy, and other emotions.

Mazu Daoyi

A Zen Master of Tang Dynasty, Mazu Daoyi once said to his students, "You should all firmly believe that your own heart is the buddha, that this heart is the buddha. Master Bodhidharma journeyed all the way from India to China to transmit this supreme truth to enable all of you to attain enlightenment."

One of his famous disciples, Damei asked Mazu, "What is the buddha?"

Mazu responded, "The heart is the buddha."

Sometimes later, a monk asked, "Why did the Master say that the 'Heart is the buddha'?"

Mazu responded, "So, the child would stop crying."

The monk inquired, "What do you say after the child stops crying?"

Mazu answered, "I would tell him, 'No heart, no buddha.'"

The monk said, "If there were a third kind of person who asked the question?"

Mazu said, "I would tell him that is also 'not object.'" ("not buddha, not heart, and not object")

The monk asked, "What if someone was between the first and second kind of person asked the question?"

Mazu said, "I would tell him to experience the absolute reality."

Mind Only

See *Yogacara*.

Mount Wutai

A mountain range in China reputed to be the residence of Manjushri Bodhisattva where Manjushri has been known to manifest himself to devotees.

Mudra (Sanskrit, literally "Seal")

It is an expression of hands and fingers that corresponds to the enlightened body of the three secrets of tathagata (enlightened body, speech, and mind). In meditational practices, forming mudra assists the practitioner to correspond his body with enlightened body of the personal deity. In application, mudra acts as a seal reinforcing the power of mantra and visualization.

Nagarjuna

Born into a Brahmin family in southern India, he could commit any sutra to memory. After renunciation, he completed reading the three Buddhist canons in ninety days and gained insight into all profound doctrines. Since his ancestral link could be traced to the nagas or dragons of northern India, he was able to enter the dragon palace under the ocean and study all the Mahayana scriptures that were being kept there, make copies, and bring these scriptures back to the human world. This was the reason why Mahayana Buddhism flourished. He was taught by Vajrasattva and from these teachings he wrote the *Madhyamaka Sastra*, which later became the most important sastra for the Three Sastras School (Madhyamaka School in China). Since he received the lineage from Vajrasattva, many sects of the Vajrayana tradition named him as its founder.

-N-

Nirvana

Sanskrit for state beyond sorrow. It refers to the permanent end to all sufferings.

No birth and no cessation

A description of absolute reality. Since all things are empty of inherent existence, from the perspective of absolute reality, there was no birth and no cessation.

Non-arising

See "*No birth and No cessation.*"

Not Abiding Anywhere

A translation of Sanskrit apratisthita. This is a characteristic of intrinsic awareness of recognizing everything in their intrinsic nature of being empty of inherent existence. Hence, enlightened beings are not bound or restricted to any place. Not abiding anywhere is the infinite spontaneity of being everywhere.

-O-

Obscuring Hindrances
Dissonant emotions, habitual tendencies, belief in the inherent existence of self, holding the belief that phenomena are real, hindrances of worldly knowledge of differentiating what is seemingly real, and the three poisons of greed, anger, and ignorance.

-P-

Padmakumara
The bliss body of Living Buddha Lian-sheng, a great fortune-bestowing and hindrance removing bodhisattva.

Perfection Stage
Also translated as completion stage, perfection stage is second and final phase of Vajrayana cultivation to attain buddhahood in the present body. The practices of the perfection stage involve directing the movement of qi (vital energy) and bodhicitta (vital fluid) within the central channel of the body.

Personal Deity
Also known as meditational deity and principal deity, a personal deity is a buddha or bodhisattva who serves as the model for the practitioner to emulate.

Prajnaparamita
The perfection of wisdom or perfect insight of reality.

Pure Land
Also translated as buddha field or pure realm, a pure land is a pure realm created by a buddha through his realization for his devotees. In the pure land, devotees can focus on their spiritual cultivation and progress towards enlightenment.

-Q-

Qi
Qi is Chinese for vital energy of the body (the Sanskrit word is prana and is translated as "wind") which, when properly cultivated, will enable the cultivator to access higher levels of spiritual awakening.

-R-

Rainbow Body
See *Great Perfection.*

Ratnasambhava Buddha (Sanskrit, literally "Jewel-born One")
One of the Five Wisdom Buddhas and Lord of the Jewel family. Ratnasambhava embodies the Wisdom of Equality in Nature, by which feelings are transformed into love and compassion and is the antidote to pride. He is associated with the element earth, the color of yellow and southern direction.

Realization
See *Enlightenment.*

-S-

Sadhana
A means of accomplishment, a sequence of prescribed visualization,

mudra, and mantra performed to cut through mental obscuration.

Saha World (Sanskrit, literally "Endure")
The Buddha called our world system the Saha World because sentient beings in this world patiently endure immeasurable hardships while pursuing fleeting illusory happiness. The beginningless delusion obscures their minds from recognizing their sufferings and how to achieve liberation.

Samadhi (Sanskrit, literally "Make firm")
Referring to the state one achieves in meditation where the boundary between the practitioner and the object of the meditation (e.g. the personal deity) vanishes.

Samsara (Sanskrit, literally "Journey")
Referring to cyclic existence and the associated sufferings in Buddhist terminology. In Mahayana writings, samara refers to the phenomenal universe and is considered to be the same as nirvana. Although this unity of samsara and nirvana seems contradictory, Mahayana tradition like Yogacara School teaches that everything is the play of the mind. Hence, samsara and nirvana are just mental labels without any real substances. Therefore, if you ignore the physical aspects of these mental labels and only consider their true nature, samsara and nirvana are one and the same.

Sangha (Sanskrit, literally "Community," "Assembly," or "Association with a Common Goal")
Traditionally, it refers to the monastic Sangha of noble ordained monks and nuns who are responsible for teaching, spreading and maintaining the teachings of the Buddha. Its usage has broadened to include Buddhist followers in general, including laity.

Sariputra
Originally known as Upatisya, he was the son of a Brahman scholar. Before taking refuge in the Buddha, he had already acquired many students of his own, and eventually led three hundred and fifty students to take refuge in the Buddha. He was renowned for his great wisdom, a primary disciple of Shakyamuni Buddha, and the person most trusted by the Buddha. He followed the Buddha for more than forty years, during which not one single thought of displeasure or dissatisfaction with the Buddha arose in him. He entered into the tranquil realm of nirvana before the Buddha did.

Shakyamuni Buddha Holding Up a Flower
The lineage of Zen Buddhism started with one of the Buddha's teachings given at Vulture Peak Mountain. The Buddha held up a flower. No one in the assembly understood the meaning except Mahakasyapa (one of Shakyamuni's principal disciples) who smiled at the Buddha. This was the beginning of Zen Buddhism, the transmission outside of scripture.

Siddhartha Gautama
The original name of Shakyamuni Buddha before his enlightenment.

Siddhi (Sanskrit, literally "Accomplishment" or "Attainment")
Its usage in Buddhism is in the spiritual sense. Accomplishment comes in the form of supreme or mundane accomplishment. The supreme accomplishment is the attainment of buddhahood and enlightenment. The mundane accomplishment is the six magical powers that arise as the result of Buddhist spiritual training.

Six Consciousnesses (Six Indriyas)
Perceptions and discernments of the six sensory organs (six roots) which shape what we perceive reality to be. The six consciousnesses

are: (1) sight-consciousness; (2) hearing-consciousness; (3) smell-consciousness; (4) taste-consciousness; (5) body-consciousness; (6) thought-consciousness.

Six Defilements
The six defilements are greed, anger, ignorance, arrogance, doubt, and false view.

Six Paramitas
The six perfections or six traits which all spiritual cultivators should perfect. These traits are: generosity, discipline, patience, diligence, meditation, and wisdom.

Six Roots
The six sensory organs of eyes, ears, nose, tongue, body, and mind through which we perceive the material universe.

Six Yogas of Naropa
These are a collection of perfection stage practices which are: Inner fire (tummo), illusory body (Gyulu) dream yoga (milam), clear light (osel), consciousness transference (Phowa), and bardo.

Skillful Means
Also translated as "expedient means" or "skill in means," "skillful means" is translation of the Sanskrit word upaya. The term, skillful means, refers to adjusting the teachings according to the capacities and the needs of the audience while applying perfect insight of emptiness and compassion to guide them toward enlightenment.

Sravaka (Sanskrit, literally "Hearer")
One who attains liberation being a disciple and hearing the teachings of a buddha.

Substantiality

Something that is permanent, exists inherently, and its existence is independent of other factors. Buddhist analysis shows that all things lack substantiality (empty of substantiality) and are all empty of inherent existence.

Sutra

Meaning "a thread that keeps things together" in Sanskrit which is the metaphor for a set of rules and principles. In Buddhism, sutras are discourses given by the Shakyamuni Buddha. Its usage has broadened to designate discourses by other buddhas such as the *Mahavairocana Sutra* or other highly regarded sacred Buddhist texts, such as the *Platform Sutra*.

Sutra Buddhism

Also referred to as Sutrayana and Exoteric Buddhism, Sutra Buddhism are branches of Buddhism that teaches the truths which the Buddha taught openly to the public. This terminology is used to distinguish teachings that were open to the public from esoteric teachings that were revealed to high capacity disciples in private. Vajrayana Schools see teachings of Sutra Buddhism as foundation of Buddhist cultivation and its practices as accumulating causes that leads to liberation. Only when the students have completed their training in Sutra Buddhism may they commence learning the Tantra System.

-T-

Tantra (Sanskrit, literally "Continuum")

In Buddhist terminology, a tantra is a Buddhist scripture of Vajrayana practices.

Tathagata
Sanskrit for "Thus who have gone" and "Thus who have come." It is one of ten titles of buddhas.

Three Bodies of a Buddha
The doctrine of trikaya, which in Sanskrit means "three bodies." The three bodies of a buddha are the dharma body, the bliss body, and the emanation body. The dharma body of buddha is a buddha in its absolute state like Mahavairocana. The dharma body is the true form of a buddha. The true form of a buddha is beyond even the perceptions and comprehension of the bodhisattva. As a bridge, the bliss body buddha, such as Amitabha Buddha, is projected by the dharma body buddha to communicate and teach bodhisattvas and gods. These buddhas are beings of radiant body. The emanation body is projected by the bliss body buddha to the human world to teach and communicate with sentient beings since most sentient beings are not able to perceive a buddha in its bliss body form.

Three Realms
The Desire Realm, Form Realm, and Formless Realm. It is another way in which Buddhism distinguishes between different modes of existence. The Desire Realm encompasses the hell realm, animal realm, human realm, asura realm, and heavens up to the Parmanirmitavasavartin Heavens. The common characteristic is that the beings in this realm are dominated by desire. The Form Realm encompasses the four dhyani heavens. The beings in this realm have renounced desire but they still have not renounced form. So, the beings in these heavens still have form and reside in celestial palaces. The Formless Realm encompasses the four formless heavens. The beings in this realm have renounced both desire and form to exist in states of formlessness.

Three Turnings of the Dharma Wheel
A metaphor for transmission of Buddhist teaching. The "Three Turnings of the Dharma Wheel" delineates the three vehicles of Buddhist teachings. The first turning of dharma wheel was the teaching of the Four Noble Truths and liberation through the noble eight-folded path. The second turning of dharma was the perfection of the wisdom sutras. The third turning was the teaching of Buddhist tantra such as the *Mahavairocana Sutra*.

Transmigration
Sentient beings are bound to the six realms of rebirth life after life as result of their karmas. They transmigrate life after life in one realm or transmigrate from one realm to another depending on their karmic deeds.

Tripitaka (Sanskrit, literally "Three Baskets")
The scared Buddhist scriptures texts, which can be divided into three categories: Vinaya, Sutra, and Abhidharma. Vinayas are the precepts for Buddhists to follow. Sutras are discourses of the Buddha. Abhidharma are commentaries on Buddhist teachings.

Tummo Fire
Inner heat yoga and a practice of the perfection stage. In this practice, a warm energy is guided from the navel center to travel up the central channel. The goal is to untangle the knots in the central channel gaining access to mind of clear light.

Twelve Links of Dependent Origination
The principle of dependent origination is the basis of the Buddhist worldview. The Buddha observed that all phenomena come into existence as the aggregate of many causes and conditions. Nothing comes into being independently of other factors, hence the name,

dependent origination. In this doctrine, there is no need for a creator. In the Buddhist worldview, every aspect of the physical universe comes into being as part of an infinite series of cyclic existence that have neither a beginning nor an end. In the relative sense, the Buddha observed that this infinite series of cyclic existence is made up individual cycles of Twelve Links of Dependent Origination. Each individual cycle is caused by ignorance. This ignorance is the misunderstanding of the true nature of absolute reality. This misunderstanding causes the false notion of a permanent "self," and this "self" needs to be placated, defended, and prolonged, thereby, initiating the sequence of Twelve Links of Dependent Origination. The Twelve Links are: Ignorance, motivational tendencies, consciousness, name and form, the six senses, sense impression, sensation, attachment, grasping, process of rebirth, birth, and old age and death. By reversing the fundamental ignorance skillfully, one can break out the cyclic existence and attain liberation.

Two Truths Doctrine
The truths revealed by the Buddha are divided into absolute truth and conventional truth. Absolute truth is reality as it is. Conventional truth is empirical aspect of reality as experienced by our perceptions. This conventional reality is only true with a relative frame of reference, but not true in the absolute sense. The Buddha taught conventional truths in order to bridge the gap between beings obscured by ignorance and the absolute reality.

-U-

-V-

Vajrakilaya (Sanskrit, literally "Vajra Dagger")
Aso referred to as "Phurba," or "Vajrakila," this dagger-like ritual

instrument is used in one of the Kalachakra practices. The handle can have three to four faces. The faces on the vajrakilaya are typically black, red, and white.

Vajra Master (Vajra Acharya)
A master of Vajrayana teachings who has achieved accomplishment in esoteric practices and can guide trainees to overcome spiritual obstacles toward enlightenment. In True Buddha School, the Vajra Master's are identified with yellow collars on their lama robes.

Vajrapani Bodhisattva
Lord of Secrets, this bodhisattva is the embodiment of power and skillful means. He is the one of the chief propagators of Vajrayana teachings.

Vajrayana Buddhism
Vajrayana is translated as Diamond Vehicle, Vehicle of the Indestructible reality, Vehicle of the Secret Mantra, or Adamantine Vehicle. It is also called Esoteric Buddhism, Tantrayana or Tantric Buddhism.

Among its many names, this system is called the secret mantra because the profound three secrets of the buddha (enlightened body, speech, and mind) are taught as the innate nature of all phenomena. However, this profound truth is concealed by the beginningless delusion which has obscured the minds of sentient beings and must be revealed skillfully. It is taught in secret and not shown to practitioners with mundane aspirations. It is called mantra because the three secrets are presented as it actually is which is beyond the perceptions of ordinary mind.

The Vajrayana trainings consist of two phases. In the first phase is the "generation stage" These teachings emphasize on the three secrets of the tathagatas, removing trainee's obscuration to recognize that one's own body, speech, and mind are the same as that of the enlightened body, speech, and mind of a buddha. In the second phase, the "perfection stage," the trainee learns to direct the subtle vital energy and essence within the body's energy channels to manifest great bliss, inner radiance, and emptiness. Through this experiential sequence, the obscurations of trainee are removed to recognize the innate awareness that has always been there. Through the diligent practice of Vajrayana teachings, one may dissolve the beginningless delusion and attain buddhahood within a single lifetime.

-W-

-X-

-Y-

Yogacara School (Sanskrit, literally "Practice of Yoga")
One of the major schools of Mahayana Buddhism, it is commonly called the Cittamatra (Mind Only) School as well as Vijnanavada (Way of Consciousness) and Vijnana-matra (Consciousness Only). Established by two brothers, Asanga and Vasubandhu, it was said that Asanga beseeched Maitreya Bodhisattva to reveal to him the true meaning of emptiness. In response, Maitreya Bodhisattva appeared to Asanga for five months explaining to him the meaning of emptiness which Asanga recorded down as the *Five Treatises of Maitreya*, which became the foundation of Yogacara philosophies.

The Yogacara School systematically analyzes cognition, consciousness and perceptions to overcome the ignorance that prevents one from breaking out of cyclic existence. It focuses on studying consciousness because it is the cause of cyclic existence.

The eight consciousness defined by Yogacara are: (1) eye-consciousness; (2) ear-consciousness; (3) nose-consciousness; (4) tongue-consciousness; (5) body-consciousness; (6) thought-consciousness; (7) manas-consciousness; (8) alaya-consciousness.

-Z-